At the Closing of a Day

The Diary of Sgt. Merle Alan Fisher Company B, 1st Amphibious Tractor Battalion, 1st Marine Division 1942–1944

Edited by

Gary A. Fisher

DORRANCE PUBLISHING CO., INC.
PITTSBURGH, PENNSYLVANIA 15222

Please note this book has been edited in a manner to preserve the original style, intent, and expression of the author.

ISBN: 978-1-4349-0836-0
eISBN: 978-1-4349-5590-6
Printed in the United States of America

First Printing

For more information or to order additional books, please contact:
Dorrance Publishing Co., Inc.
701 Smithfield Street
Pittsburgh, Pennsylvania 15222
U.S.A.
1-800-788-7654
www.dorrancebookstore.com

This book is dedicated to all members of the
1st Marine Division past and present.

Contents

Merle Alan Fisher, affectionately called Sonny by his parents, was born in Cleveland, Ohio, on October 13, 1919. He graduated from Charles F. Bush High School and had been employed by Fisher Foods prior to his enlistment in the Marine Corps on January 12, 1942. He trained at Parris Island, South Carolina, and New River, North Carolina, before deploying to the Pacific Theater. He participated in the following campaigns: Guadalcanal-Tulagi landings, August 7 to August 9, 1942, and the defense of Guadalcanal, Solomon Island, August 10 to December 15, 1942; Eastern New Guinea Operation, October 15, 1942, to December 25, 1943; Bismarck Archipelago Operation, December 26, 1943, to April 25. 1944; Peleliu, Palau Islands, September 15 to September 25, 1944.

Sgt. Fisher was wounded during the Peleliu campaign and died of his wounds aboard the USS *Solace* on September 26, 1944. He was awarded the Purple Heart, Presidential Unit Citation with one star, Asiatic Pacific Campaign Medal with four Bronze Stars, and the World War II Victory Medal.

This is his diary. It begins on June 6, 1942, just prior to departing the Norfolk Navy Yard, Virginia, in a convoy to Wellington, New Zealand, and ends on September 24, 1944.

There sleeps tonight across the sea on the Isle of Guadalcanal.
A golden haired young leatherneck who did his part so well.
He died while in a battle at the closing of a day.
And just before he closed his eyes his comrades heard him say.
When I'm gone please write to my mother. The mother I love so well.
That I died thinking of her on the Isle of Guadalcanal.
When I'm gone please write to my country how we swore before we fell.
That old glory would soon be waving on the Isle of Guadalcanal.

Merle Fisher was an amateur artist. On a signal flag, he drew a picture of Guadalcanal combat and included this poem in the drawing.

Chapter 1

Convoy 1

Saturday, June 6, 1942

Last liberty, went out with Val and Collins—and I do mean out!

Sunday, June 7, 1942

Woke up with a bad hand, a cut head, and no hair. Almost a tattoo. Left New River at 6:30 P.M. A lovely ride was had by all. Beginning of a trip to???? Wonder where I will be a year from now.

Monday, June 8, 1942

Arrived at Norfolk Navy Yard, Virginia, at 6:30 A.M. Boarded the ship *Alcyone* at 7:15 A.M. No liberty! No letter writing! Started work at 1:00 P.M. Sleeping quarters very crowded. Aft one five-inch gun, two three-inch guns midship, anti-aircraft guns, spotlight. *Juke Box Jenny* picture show.

Tuesday, June 9, 1942

Second day aboard ship, still at port and NO liberty! Confined to ship! Work easier and less hours. Ship loaded with TNT, dynamite, and munitions, gas, and all high explosives.

Wednesday, June 10, 1942

Pulled up anchor and set sail at 7:15 A.M. to where???? Big convoy. Three other supply ships and five destroyers that I know of. Three flags up top, blue and white checkered. Middle, white with square of red in the center bottom half; half white and half blue. Sailors sounding depth—cool and foggy. Got life belt at 9:30 A.M. Orders are to wear whenever on deck. Saw *St. Louis Blues.*

Thursday, June 11, 1942

Second day at sea. 4:00 A.M. siren blew to man battle stations; a battleship on the horizon, but it was a false alarm, as it was an allied ship. Late in the afternoon another ship was sighted, but it wasn't an enemy ship. Didn't come very close to it. We have three other supply ships with us and five destroyers with us for protection. Got quite a sunburn on deck. Water very pretty, dark blue, and the way the water cuts away from the ship was beautiful in color. We were warned today that we were in dangerous waters. No smoking on deck after dark. Below, blue lights after dark. Nearly broke my neck a couple of times.

Friday, June 12, 1942

Saw my first sight of flying fish today. Submarine reported 200 miles north of us today and had me worried for awhile, but I do wish we could see some action. Still headed south. Wednesday we started north; thought we were going to Ireland, but since then we have been going south. Around 4:00 P.M. we were off the coast of Florida. We are now near Cuba; 9.15 P.M. The sunset tonight was at 8:30 P.M. and it sure was a beautiful sight to see. Received address cards today, but you just get one. One side your parents' address and the other your name. Can't say any more than that and in case of capture will be destroyed.

Saturday, June 13, 1942

Sixth day aboard ship and fourth day at sea. Saw *Midnight* Friday night but the picture machine broke on the fourth reel. Found out yesterday my address is: Marine Corps Unit No. 140, % of Postmaster, San Francisco, California. Saturday inspection day aboard ship. At 3:00 P.M. destroyers started dropping depth bombs and course of convoy was changed. Our ship signaled the destroyers and was answered. Our forward guns were uncovered and manned. But that was all we were told—nothing.

Sunday, June 14, 1942

See most of the fellows in shorts now, it's darned hot. Yesterday I cut the legs off a pair of white pants. I hemmed them and I did get my legs burned. At 4:00 P.M. we passed Puerto Rico, at 6:00 P.M. we are nearing San Juan. Came upon gulls and a patch of oil on the surface either from a tanker or sub that had been sunk.

Monday, June 15, 1942

Last night we passed a life boat adrift in the ocean, but we didn't stop to pick it up. Today we are celebrating the ship's first birthday as it is just a year ago today it was commissioned in the Navy. Heat is terrible. Had turkey, got two packs of Chesterfields free. Sunsets at night are really beautiful. Slept on deck, can't stand it below. Heat is terrific. Darkened ship at 8:00 P.M. One single row of cots and two double rows four high. First about one foot off deck. About two feet in between cots and about three feet passageway. When two meet, you have to squeeze to get by. Just a week on board ship.

Tuesday, June 16, 1942

Went to get my shirt and found out somebody had cut out a big piece of it. Just one destroyer with us as we broke down early this morning; the convoy went on ahead. Ninth day aboard ship. Seventh day at sea. Changed time again; set watch back an hour so it makes time just right again. Caught up with convoy. It makes me feel better. It rains quite frequently down here in this tropical climate. Well, supposed to hit Panama tomorrow. In the Caribbean Sea today and went through it.

Wednesday, June 17, 1942

Land sighted at dawn. Came to the Panama Canal at 9:00 A.M. Standard Time, 10:00 A.M. War Time. Hit first lock at 9:25 A.M. Standard Time. Each lock takes 9 ½ minutes to fill four feet per minute, 38 feet all told and went through three locks. Now approaching Culebra but at 12:35 heat is quite bad. Just rained hard but it only lasted five minutes. As we approach Culebra, the highest mountain face is bare coloring block tinted with red with dense growth on top. Canal is 37.8 miles long. Brass plate in face of mountain, "1907," where and when the canal was completed. Approached and went through fourth lock; took eight minutes to fill up thirty feet of water.

Friday, June 19, 1942

We got the word today that we are going to Wellington, New Zealand. Second day in the Pacific. Weather warm, strong wind and getting rough. Quite a few of the boys are seasick, and now are getting sick all the time. Keep having calls to abandon ship. All are assigned to different life boats and rafts. Fifty-one in my raft. Fog horn blows one, means right turn. Two, left turn. Changed time again today. Add one hour. Weather bad. Nobody allowed on deck. Hit a bad squall. Raining hard and very rough.

Saturday, June 20, 1942

Third day in Pacific. Weather still bad. Raining and cool. Sea rough. Water coming over the side and on deck. Still have a long journey ahead of us. From Panama it's nearly 7,000 miles from New York, its 9,000 miles (a long ways) from home and still going further. Also sharks were sighted in quite a few numbers. Four cargo ships:

USS *Alcyone*
USS *Libra*
USS *Alchiba*
USS *Mizar*

Sunday, June 21, 1942

Thirteenth day aboard ship, still a little rough. Weather a little cool. We saw a four-motored bomber fly over us today. Played cards today and lost 75 cents playing poker. The shellbacks are getting ready to give us pollywogs the works tomorrow when we cross the equator. It's an old Navy custom and demands quite a celebration. The pollywogs just gave the shellbacks a bath in the office and turned a fire hose on them. The captain just said any more demonstrations of that sort and it would be considered mutiny on the high seas.

Monday, June 22, 1942

Well, I finally got it today, that is, my initiation. I am no longer a pollywog but a full-fledged shellback. Just I had to sit down on the deck in about six inches of water. Next I had to crawl about twenty yards through the water on my hands and knees with fellows standing on each side of me with paddles hitting me where you sit, and with wet pants it didn't ease the pain any. Next I had to crawl over to an old salt and suck on a milk bottle with the awfulest-tasting stuff. Then I had to kiss his tit. Then I crawled over to another fellow and had to kiss his bare foot. Then I was taken and put in the electric chair. Fed a piece of awful hot and rotten cake. Then grease was put in my hair and limburger cheese smeared in my face. Next I had to crawl over to the barber, but as my hair had been already cut off, there was nothing to cut off. Then I crawled through the line of boys and paddles to a canvas which was about 15 yards long. They turned the fire hose on in the canvas and I had to crawl through it receiving swats. When I emerged from the canvas, I found a line about 25 to 30 feet long which I had to go through. I can still feel them hitting me on my sitter.

The ceremony lasted from morning until supper time, about 5:30 P.M. or 6:00 P.M. Time keeps changing every day; lights went out at 6:45 P.M. That's when they darken ship.

Tuesday, June 23, 1942

Everything O.K. Nice and warm. Really is beautiful day but the ship is really rolling today. The boys were practicing with the anti-aircraft guns today. Their hits averaged one out of four. In the evening we saw the picture, *Shop around the Corner,* with James Stewart and Margaret Sullivan.

Wednesday, June 24, 1942

Time changed again. You can't keep up with it. More practice today with the anti-aircraft guns. Pacific is very rough, ship rolls from port to starboard. Began striking bells at 4, 8, 12, they strike eight bells and start out on the half hour after with one and keep adding one each half hour until eight is reached and then start over again. We're supposed to meet a convoy tomorrow.

Thursday, June 25, 1942

Received my certificate to show I'm a shellback and that I have crossed the equator. Haven't met the convoy yet. Life aboard ship is beginning to get very monotonous. Fellows are beginning to get on each other's nerves, nothing to do for amusement except movies every third night. Bob Bernie's birthday today. Collins and I bought him a carton of cigarettes and Tebbe made him a cake. Pacific is getting rougher every day. Yesterday, they had an earthquake in Wellington, New Zealand, our destination.

Friday, June 26, 1942

Wasn't Bob's birthday yesterday; somebody was stringing us along. Supposed to hit Pago Pago tomorrow or Sunday. A submarine was sighted yesterday but it retreated. Other convoy hasn't been sighted as yet. Passed oil spot where submarine had been sunk sometime before. Sharks were seen today. Trips getting more dangerous every day. Starting yesterday morning, everybody has to get up at 6:00 A.M. in case we are attacked at dawn. More precaution is being taken all the time.

Saturday, June 27, 1942

Nothing much doing. Still at sea. Very hot, days dragging and monotony growing.

Sunday, June 28, 1942

Saw a couple of bombers take off from the cruiser and go out of sight. Received word that we could write, as airmail is going to be picked up Tuesday.

Monday, June 29, 1942

Played poker with the boys and lost naturally. We're supposed to reach Tahiti tomorrow. Weather is very hot. Ocean is the calmest it has been since we left Panama. Saw sea gulls so we must be getting near land. Cruiser is supposed to leave us at Tahiti. We're supposed to meet up with a convoy there. Evening just a nice full moon on the Pacific.

Tuesday, June 30, 1942

Beautiful sunrise in the morning. Saw a battleship around 10:15 A.M.—must have been an allied—as we proceeded on our course.

Wednesday, July 1, 1942

Weather still very warm. Getting browner every day. Light shorter every day. Gets dark now at about 6:30 P.M. At 1:30 A.M. today the can (destroyer) came alongside of us and took our mail and a few boxes of fruit. It sure was a sight to see the way it cut through the water with its four forward guns bristling. Just the cruiser with us now and no protection except the cruiser. We're supposed to meet a convoy but I have my doubts. Tebbe took a shower today and used soap. He also eats a mixed variety of shit.

Thursday, July 2, 1942

Met another convoy early this morning. Got a couple of English ships escorting us now. Read *Arizona Sons of the Saddle*, got another book, *Navy Blue and Gold*. British cruiser has one airplane on it and sticks pretty close to us.

Friday, July 3, 1942

Saw a double rainbow this morning. First time I ever saw one in my life. Raining all day long. Weather rough. Ship rolling an awful lot all day long. Had an inspection of sea bags for stolen clothing. Nothing found.

Saturday, July 4, 1942

Decoration Day—so they say. Had turkey, baked ham, potatoes, lemonade, and two packages of cigarettes. Saw four seagulls today. Also, Collins and I were told to prepare to take an examination for field cook at 2:00 P.M. Collins quit smoking. Finished *Phantom Pass*, got another book, *The Redlander.* Weather getting cooler. Orders are we are to disembark in greens. Clock still being changed 25 minutes every day. Collins and I slept in our own bunk for the first time in almost three weeks.

Sunday, July 5, 1942

Weather roughest it's been in the whole trip. Woke up around 4:00 A.M. when it was real rough to the sound of three men falling out of their sack. In the galley, the frying pans went off the stoves, dishes fell and broke, and everything was a general mess. In the afternoon a storm came up. It started raining and got rougher—if possible. Weather growing colder. Finished reading *The Redlander.*

Monday, July 6, 1942

Finished reading *Flying Colors.* Weather still getting cooler, dark, dismal day. Ship broke down around 10:00 A.M. but they soon had it repaired and on our way again. No time change yesterday or today. Everybody wearing winter uniforms.

Tuesday, July 7, 1942

Issued combat jackets. Men on watch wearing overcoats—sailors wearing pea coats. Heat turned on today in our sleeping quarters. Nearing our destination, New Zealand. Finished *Bright Star of Danger.* Can't take out any more library books. Weather still dark and dismal, old Pacific quite rough. You walk around like a drunkard on account of the ship's rolling. Seems years ago we left instead of a little over a month.

Wednesday, July 8, 1942

Our sister ship broke down last night and is still broke down at 1:00 A.M. We're just circling around her waiting for them to get it repaired so we can get under way. Guess we'll be a few days late as we've lost one day, which is today. We're just circling around it. Read *Turn Loose Your Wolf.*

Thursday, July 9, 1942

Got under way around 6:00 P.M. last night. Orders: "Full Speed Ahead and a Straight Course, No Zigzaggin." Weather cool and clear and ocean not nearly as rough as it was. Saw porpoises playing and sea hawks were plentiful. Radio man told us Great Britain and United States were invading Italy. Saw a large white duck today.

Friday, July 10, 1942

This is gone until we come back as this is the day we skip.

Saturday, July 11, 1942

Land sighted at dawn; orders are to have our packs ready tomorrow morning right after breakfast. Seagulls and sea hawks are numerous. Will disembark either Sunday or Monday. Country very mountainous from appearances. Anchored at approximately five o'clock. Getting rough as we came along the coast. The wind is awfully hot and strong. Turned in our life belts at 4:20 P.M.

Wellington 2

Sunday, July 12, 1942

Chow early started at six o'clock. First morning the horn didn't sound; what a relief. In the harbor. Got a good look at it this morning when it was light. Got under way at 8:00 A.M. and docked up. Received liberty and went to Wellington. Buildings quite old. No drinks on Sunday. Awful lot of servicemen, limey soldiers, and air force. All stores close at 6:00 P.M. City very dark on account of the war. No street lights. Saw Wallace Berry in *Sound of the Bugle,* cost 1/6. Like trying to find your way about ship after it's darkened. Saw quite a few pretty women. Saw some of the buildings wrecked by the earthquake.

Monday, July 13, 1942

Leaving with just a heavy pack. Sea bags and blanket rolls are going to be left and stored. Sold a fountain pen $1.00, two pair khaki pants $1.50, one shirt 50 cents, green overseas cap 50 cents. Going on maneuvers but not fun. Vast conversion of troops here. Expect to go on board a transport either today or tomorrow. No more liberty. All liberty has been canceled. Guess we're going to leave New Zealand. Still raining and quite cold. Quarters are awfully cramped.

Tuesday, July 14, 1942

Still aboard the *Alcyone.* Weather is still cold and raining. Went to Wellington for liberty. Sure had a good time. Saw Valincourt. Got my watch fixed with an unbreakable crystal for 42 cents. Met Reta. Saw *Yank on the*

Burma Road. Had brandy, Scotch, beer, half and half ginger beer. Signed the payroll for $25.00.

Wednesday, July 15, 1942

Cashed and ready to go. Going on the *Barnett.* Left the USS *Alcyone* and went aboard the USS *Barnett.* Collins and Davis and I are still together with Bernie and Tebbe. Chow is lousy. Twelve of us in our quarters. Got paid $25.00. Shows and food are quite reasonable.

Thursday, July 16, 1942

Got two shots today; one in each arm. Went on liberty. Met Reta and took her out again. My buddy Collins got drunk. Reta gave me her picture. A lot of the fellows have so much money they don't know what to do with it. They have women carrying the mail, driving mail trucks, taxi cabs, working in the factories and in all the stores and hotels, etc.

Friday, July 17, 1942

Got put on a working party first thing this morning. No liberty tonight. Felt awful sick all day long from those shots yesterday. Saw Harry Wisner, my ex-assistant D.I. from Parris Island. He's on the same ship as I am, the USS *Barnett.* Roll call every morning now. We're supposed to get another shot in the arm today but it was called off.

Saturday, July 18, 1942

Saw Ike and got my half dollar. Also saw Boyela and got my $10.00. Got another shot today; this was typhoid. The other two, one was for cholera and the other a tetanus. Got through work at 7:15 P.M. The USS *Alcyone* pulled out today. No liberty. Collins sent home $50.00 today.

Sunday, July 19, 1942

Got liberty and we all went ashore. I also got a pair of new shoes and working shoes. Went and had supper then went to church. After church we had something to eat and then walked some girls home. Loaded all our galley equipment aboard ship; also had rifle inspection and inspection of quarters.

Monday, July 20, 1942

My cold is getting worse. We went on a hike today up in the mountains with rifles, belts, bayonets, dungarees. Had inspection of quarters. Ship all loaded now. Supposed to pull out tomorrow. All liberty for Marines was canceled today at 4:00 P.M. Won a dollar playing cards.

Tuesday, July 21, 1942

Pulled up anchor and anchored out in the bay. Still feeling pretty bad. Got issued life belts at 10:00 A.M. Played cards and lost a couple of dollars. Saw Harry again. Ship darkened at around six o'clock.

Fiji Island Maneuvers 3

Wednesday, July 22, 1942

Got under way early this morning. Have quite a convoy with us this time. Got vaccinated for smallpox. No more smoking in compartments. Sick all day long. Collins, Davis, and Goldman went to work in the galley. Don't know where we are going now. Ship darkened at 5:30 P.M.

Thursday, July 23, 1942

Roll call at 8:30 A.M. now instead of 8:00 A.M. Feel a little better today. Chow aboard ship sure is lousy. Worst I've had since I've been in the service. I counted ten troop ships this morning all told. We have 26 ships that include cruisers, destroyers, and troop ships and we also have planes. The number I don't know. Second day out from New Zealand.

Friday, July 24, 1942

Third day out from New Zealand. Roll call, musters, abandon ship. No roll call this morning; weather too rough. Really got rough weather this morning. Orders are to stay below in quarters as it's so stormy. All Marines are forbidden to go up on deck. Got another shot. Won about $6.00 in New Zealand money. Food is like gold. Offered fellows $1.00 for a dip of ice cream and couldn't buy it. As much as a $1.00 has been offered for an orange but you can't buy them. They wouldn't sell for any money. *But* if you're a sailor you can get more than one candy bar and buy anything you need.

Saturday, July 25, 1942

Had our vaccinations checked. Mine's good; it took O.K. Roll call this morning. Weather is still awfully rough. An awful lot of the men are seasick. They're supposed to land tomorrow. Men sleeping all over on deck, in the passageways, engine room, wherever they can find space to lay down as the ship is so crowded, there just isn't enough bunks. Took on mail today from destroyer number 330. Had rifle inspection today by Captain Ruthlinger. I got called for either dirty or rusty rifle barrel. To report to him tomorrow morning at 8:15 A.M. Maybe I did gain 30 pounds since I came in the service. It's a cinch, if I stay aboard here much longer, I'll lose that and more. Candy limited one bar to a man.

Sunday, July 26, 1942

Reading *Mission to Moscow.* We have rice with nothing to put on it and oatmeal with no milk. Weather getting warmer. Orders today are khaki shirts, caps. Ocean not very rough, really a beautiful day. Now they tell us we're supposed to land Tuesday. Passed another convoy with 20 ships. They had an aircraft carrier with them. It's supposed to be a British convoy. We started out with 26 ships and still have that many as far as I know. Lost playing cards: $8.00? Captain had all men except the cooks up on deck to tell about getting ready to make landing party.

Monday, July 27, 1942

Yesterday that convoy went around back of us and joined up with us. We now have 66 ships in all including two battleships, and one aircraft carrier. Got a pack of cigarettes and one bar of candy today. Saw and passed several islands today. The boys go over the side tomorrow to make landing parties. Just light combat packs.

Tuesday, July 28, 1942

Anchored ship at one of the Fiji Islands. Lowered boats and tank lighters and tanks for practice landings but they weren't carried out. Pulled up anchor and shoved off. Not allowed to go up on deck from now on without a helmet. Colonel's orders.

Wednesday, July 29, 1942

Anchored at one large island, called Koro, in the morning. Weather is very warm and cloudy. Awfully hot below deck. Orders are to stay in our quarters. Any kind of reading material very scarce, and bought with much anticipation. Card games can be found going on at all times and all over the ship as there isn't anything they can do. Captain gave us a talk on chemical warfare, how to take cover and protect ourselves. Use soap on your body after mustard gas.

Thursday, July 30, 1942

Still on maneuvers. Most of the men went over the side today. That is, all except our outfit. Went to sick bay for jock strap itch. Some of the ships practiced firing their guns. Huts can be made out on the island. No mail going out on the island. As yet, none has come in. Awfully hot. Sweated all day long something awful. Our outfit is supposed to go over the side tomorrow.

Friday, July 31, 1942

Weather very warm. All day was spent loading ammunition belts; .30 caliber and .50 caliber; 76,000 rounds were loaded. Two hundred fifty rounds in .30 caliber belt and ten boxes of 250 rounds for each .30 caliber machine gun. Planes were practicing dive bombings on the ships. Sailors making the ship ready for sea. Also got a free bar of candy today for some unknown reason. Sent a letter to Jeanne today. Sighted a very large shark off of the port side of the ship around 2:30 P.M.

Destination Guadalcanal 4

Saturday, August 1, 1942

7:30 A.M. we pulled up anchor and left the Islands. Maneuvers are for the real thing now. Headed for the Solomon Islands; (what-a-canal) is the island we're going to take from the Japs. Planes are supposed to be bombing the island now. We're supposed to be there by the middle of next week. All ammunition belts are loaded now, .50 caliber and .30 caliber. Passed an awful big island around 4:30 P.M. Preparations are being made for immediate attack upon arrival.

Sunday, August 2, 1942

Our outfit received cards and a few games from the chaplain aboard ship. The islands we are going to take are Guadalcanal Islands. Played cards all day long. Also got a haircut. Sergeant Baily inspected our gear looking for a radio which has been sending out sound messages. As yet, it hasn't been located. Heat rash coming along much better. Planes were flying in formation and practicing dive bombing. Ammunition has been brought down and put in our compartments to be issued out for our rifles. Ocean calm and it was quite hot in the afternoon. Took on mail from the *McCudy*.

Monday, August 3, 1942

Captain called me down this morning. Itch is still bad. Passed one of the Solomon Islands today. Time was changed last night at 6:00 P.M. Lost an hour. Set the clock back to 5:00 P.M. Top sergeant was censoring all wallets today. Only identification allowed on your personage is dog tags. In the press wireless today, it was stated that the Japanese extended their hold on the Solomon

Islands by seizing Guadalcanal Islands. That is the island we are headed for. Expect to arrive there in the next two days. Also, the radio set aboard ship was found. Don't know what happened to the owner. Won $8.40 playing poker today.

Tuesday, August 4, 1942

Free candy and two packages of cigarettes. They gave us the word today that we are going to attack Friday, August 7th. Just eight months after the tragic attack on Pearl Harbor, Dec. 7th, 1941. We're to get all the dope tomorrow afternoon at 1:00 P.M.

Wednesday, August 5, 1942

Issued us headnets, mosquito headnets, this morning. Leave one pack behind. It has to be ready tomorrow with our blankets and shelter half. Captain gave us all the dope today. Studied the maps where headquarters will be and where we are to land and where we proceed from there. Got two packs of cigarettes and bar of candy free today. Men practiced firing .50 caliber and .30 caliber machine guns. Planes practiced dive bombing. Foster owes me $17.00 and Jeff Cost owes me $3.00.

Thursday, August 6, 1942

The day before the big drive. Busy all day long. Packed our greens away in the tractors. Our lower packs and blankets and shelter half stored away above deck. Issued four cans of rations and three chocolate field bar rations plus 220 rounds of ammunition. One hundred rounds of ammunition for our cartridge belt and two bandoliers, consisting of 60 rounds each. Reveille is at 3:30 A.M. tomorrow morning. Also have mosquito netting with poncho. Go ashore with rifle, belt, bayonet, light combat pack, ha.

Guadalcanal Campaign 5

Friday, August 7, 1942

Zero day. Got up at 3:00 A.M. Attack starts at dawn. Sunk one Japanese ship. Cruisers and destroyers laid down a barrage. First wave went over the side at 8:30 A.M. Unloaded about 50 tons of .30 caliber ammunition from the hold when 15 Jap planes flew over and started bombing us. Two were shot down. Second plane attack came at 3:00 P.M. Seven planes came over, one was shot down. I don't mind saying I was pretty scared. Loaded six tons of potatoes and two tons of onions. Twenty-four hundred pounds of butter; also cheese and canned luncheon meat. Started work at 5:00 A.M. 8:00 P.M. now and still working. Loaded 99 bags of coffee and 50 bags of sugar. 1:00 A.M.: still working. 157 cases of can milk, 150 cases of tomatoes, 32 of figs. Forty cases of peas, 70 of beans, 30 of corn. Hope we're through by dawn as we're expecting another air attack then. This sure isn't my idea of a good time.

Saturday, August 8, 1942

Stopped working this morning at 5:00 A.M. Yesterday seven planes were shot down and one was hit. Don't know if it went down by our ship later or not. One plane was shot down by our ship by a 3" gun, or aft gun. The destroyer next to us was hit on the starboard quarterdeck. 11:00 A.M. They're coming again. I sure don't like Jap planes or their bombs either. They came around 12:00 P.M. Twenty-six Jap planes broke through. The ships accounted for 17 planes and our planes got two more before they got away. This ship accounted for four planes. One Jap dove his plane into the *Elliot* and set her afire. We've got four Jap prisoners aboard now from the planes. One destroyer was hit by a shell but it just damaged it. One plane lost a wing on our ship and went in the ocean alongside. He strafed the ship with his fire and broke a window.

Sunday, August 9, 1942

Around 2:00 A.M. this morning we got another warning. This time it was the Japanese fleet. Around 4:00 A.M. the all clear was sounded. Two of our men at the guns were hit by shrapnel. We finally got to the beach around 10:00 A.M. The island has a very small beach. Lots of coconut trees here and dense undergrowth. Ate some coconuts today. Sergeant Stone captured a Jap truck, Pontiac make. A lot of Jap snipers around here. Rifle shots all day long. Living on canned rations and coconuts. One man from our battalion shot. Collins in Company A. Got our gear, can't go outside of our park where we have our tractors parked. The fleet left with the troop's ships and supply ships. Taking prisoners all the time. Pickering and DeCasper; two accidents. Former had arm amputated and later, four shots in body. One in leg, chin, crotch, and elbow.

Monday, August 10, 1942

Had two air attacks by the Japs. Set up our own galley. Back with Hoff and Tebbe again. Valincourt didn't get off the ship so he went back to New Zealand. Killed a big lizard and one of the fellows killed a big snake. The place is lousy with ants, bugs, lizards, etc. Had some Jap beer, it's pretty good, too. Got some Jap money and cigarettes. Drank some Jap sake; it's pretty powerful stuff. Have our beach defense set up. Captured about 20 Jap trucks, also Jap motorcycles and bikes. The airport has been taken. Took a swim in the ocean. Worked like hell all day long. Sure living a rugged life. Sniping is very bad. Some broke through in the night and bullets were flying all night long.

Tuesday, August 11, 1942

Moved camp. We moved about five miles nearer the front. Passed a few buildings that had been struck by our shells and a lot of palm trees that had been knocked down by shells. The hills and mountains can be seen more plainly now. One of our boys captured a Jap yesterday. We're two rivers up from where we were. One river is right near us. Quite a few alligators were seen in there yesterday. Swimming is forbidden in there. Have a box of cigars and about four cartons of cigarettes which cost nothing. One of our boys captured a Jap bicycle. One fellow caught quite a few fish in the river. Some Japs surrendered and when they got close, threw some hand grenades. The natives have been very helpful to the Marine Corps in giving us information, etc. One fellow got shot by a sniper last night and one got a bayonet in him.

Wednesday, August 12, 1942

Had an air attack this morning by a few planes. They only dropped a few bombs but they didn't do any damage. Tebbe got out of the galley. Today is his last day; he goes on line duty tomorrow. Guess we're going to stay here some time, by the looks of things. We had to dig trenches in the ground to sleep in and for air attacks ... that was orders. The captain said Bernie and I had our recommendation in but it's just that they haven't come through yet. Two Japs surrendered today and said 25 men and two officers were back in the hills and would surrender if we didn't kill them. Some of our tractors got stuck in the river. Moved the galley again today; also peeled potatoes. Rode a Jap bike today and also went swimming. Got up at 4:00 A.M. and worked until 7:00 P.M. Having coffee tomorrow morning; had to pound the coffee beans with a two-by-four.

Thursday, August 13, 1942

Have an awful lot of the islands natives with us. They are being friendly and typical of tropical natives. Had to sleep in a hole on account of snipers. A submarine shelled us all to hell early this morning just before dawn this morning and twice later on in the day. Last night the Japs got 23 out of 25 men in the night. Saw some alligators again today and Collins and Davis caught some fish. Went about five miles up to get some water and got a Jap jacket and soap, opium pipe, etc. Four of our boys killed one Jap and brought three Jap prisoners. Eight of us washed in a little basin of water. Saw them get two Jap snipers today. Radio from San Francisco said "Fighting Marines have taken and are holding the Solomon Islands." Davis got some Jap sandals and pants.

Friday, August 14, 1942

The island is 90 miles by 30 miles. Yesterday we started on two meals a day, breakfast and supper. No dinner. Last night snipers were shooting .25 caliber and machine guns and flares all night long. Got a lot of Jap food today: rice, oats, hardtack, peaches, pineapple, beef, canned milk, tomatoes, carrots, bamboo roots, celery, salt, and extract lemon. Had a bombing by planes around noon. They bombed the airport and vicinity. Had an attack on the island by two submarines. They think they hit one but they're not sure. Got a chance to send a letter home tomorrow. We get two bottles of sake and one bottle of brandy, new toothbrush and some Jap candy. Some of our boys captured 175 Japs last night. Going in for a swim now as it's getting dark. The Japs amazed me with the food stored and machinery they have here. They captured a radio station worth a million dollars.

Saturday, August 15, 1942

Got the official word today that our men sunk one of the submarines yesterday. Our guns also downed one plane yesterday on the other island where our parachute troops landed; they lost around 91 men but there was over 1,000 Japs. No prisoners were taken. Had two attacks by planes today; they dropped some parachutes. Don't know if it was men or supplies. There were only three planes. Sent a letter home today. 1:00 P.M. moving now up nearer the attack. We're moving up to the airport now. Got a beautiful Japanese blanket today plus a jacket. Tenaru River is the one we are moving from; before we had our camp by the Ilu. Now we're moving up by the Lunga River and will be between the Lunga River and the Kukum River. Got moved and set up a new galley. So far everything is okay and running smooth. That is, as smooth as can be expected.

Sunday, August 16, 1942

Running under a new schedule now. Good sleeping last night; no shelling or bombing, not even snipers bothered us last night. Setting up a pretty good camp now. Best one so far but we have more to work with now. Four destroyers came in the harbor last night. Took a fresh water bath in the Kukum River around noon. We're still on two meals a day. Reveille at 6:00 A.M. Now breakfast at 9:00 A.M. and supper at 5:00 P.M. Now we have a .50 caliber antiaircraft outfit. Had a tropical rainstorm today and some more Jap clothes and chow. Got burnt today. One of the boys spilt a can of hot grease on me. Mostly on the belly though. Got half in the bag today on Jap beer and sake. A few bombs dropped today. Outside of that, everything was quiet. One fellow brought in a Jap prisoner.

Monday, August 17, 1942

We took six Jap prisoners today. Four early in the morning came into camp with a white flag and their hands up and later on in the afternoon, two more gave themselves up. Some of the other outfits got some Japs today too. Heard today that we're going to get 100 new tractors and be a combat unit and go over in the first wave on the next island we take. We're supposed to stay here for about 30 days. The radio said that in Italy the people were throwing down their arms and were refusing to fight also. Came across a lot of shrapnel and shell heads in the woods and jungle today. Went swimming in the river today. Went back in the jungle with Davis today and tried to find some Japs but we couldn't find any.

Tuesday, August 18, 1942

Altogether we got 12 Japs in our outfit yesterday. All told we got 64 prisoners yesterday. We caught a phosphorous worm last night; they're thin and look just like a regular angle worm. Sunday night Ted got drunk for the first time in his life. Ate some Japanese vermicelli; looks like spaghetti but it's made of rice. We got a cow and butchered it. We only got to keep ¾ of the cow. Saw Wales today, he's still with 1st Service Battalion. Had a bombing by eight planes (Jap). One Marine was killed and three were wounded. One of our boys got hurt pretty bad yesterday when he was cleaning his tractor motor with gas when a spark exploded the gas. He got burned pretty bad. Got a .50 caliber that went through the roof of a building and through the walls and into a tree. Radio announcement that Marines are holding the islands and cleaning it of Japs.

Wednesday, August 19, 1942

The Japs started shelling Tulagi last night and up until around 10:00 A.M. this morning we could hear the shells whistling over our heads and they sure didn't make us feel very comfortable. They're trying to make a landing party on Tulagi. Jap reports they sunk 40 American transports and are cleaning up the few Marines left on the Solomon Islands. Orders are not to leave our camp vicinity and to wear helmets, cartridge belts, gas masks, and rifle. Higgins boat with two men lost today. We hit a Jap ship; either a light cruiser or a destroyer, not certain which it was. Our company moving around tomorrow expecting a landing from the Japs. Reveille at 3:30 A.M. Tomorrow our tractors are to be ready to leave at 4:00 A.M. No more looting of any kind. Punishable by being shot.

Thursday, August 20, 1942

The Jap cruiser was sunk; the report has been confirmed. Twenty-five Japs from the cruiser landed this morning. We lost three men. Two BAR men and one rifleman. Out of the 25 Japs, we took one prisoner; an officer. The other 24 are dead. The expected attack didn't come off this morning. We're expecting a bombing today. Radio report from Australia said Japanese bombers are headed this way. Radio announcement from San Francisco gave the Amphibious Tractor Battalion the credit for taking Guadalcanal Island. Hit Parade played "Some of These Days" for the Marines on the Solomon Islands. We've really eaten enough hardtack to last the rest of my life. I don't want any rice, corned beef, beans, or fish when I get back to the States. Twenty-eight of our men went in the boondocks with two days' rations. In the river, big fish are plentiful but hard to catch. We got some planes today. We got 47 planes with Marine pilots. Wrote a letter home today; it's to go out tomorrow. Sure feel a lot better since they came here.

Friday, August 21, 1942

Hoff, Davis. and I went up to the front lines this morning and were leading the charge. Don't know how many Japs we got as a lot of others fired as we did and that was when we saw them. Saw an awful lot of dead Japs and also Marines. They had some hand-to-hand fighting before we got there. I nearly got it. A bullet just missed my head by about a foot. Davis brought back a Jap rifle and I brought back a Jap coin, and an American rising gun. Hoff brought back a few grenades and some Jap ammunition. Really had some excitement and I'll guarantee you that it's one day that I'll never forget as long as I live. We lost about 32 Marine dead and around 68 wounded. The Jap dead count was over 700 dead and one prisoner. Four of our planes met 10 Jap fighters. Two Jap planes lost; we lost none.

Saturday, August 22, 1942

Two destroyers came in late last night with supplies for us. We robbed around 30 cases of food. Hoff, Davis, Collins, Ted and Frank and myself had our hair cut off today and shaved. The Jap prisoners were kept busy burying dead Marines and making crosses for their graves. But the Japs were all thrown together in a big hole and buried in mass numbers. We got some Army Flying Fortresses today. Number unknown. Getting the lines set up and guarding the beach. We're expecting another attack by Japs either tonight or tomorrow. The boys were busy today piling up sandbags around the million-dollar radio set to protect it from air raids and shellings. The island is full of parrots and one of the fellows caught one and has it for a pet now. It's really attached to him now.

Sunday, August 23, 1942

Today was one of the most exciting days we had since landing on the island. Davis, Huff, and myself left camp around dawn. About five miles back in the jungle, we encountered some Jap sailors. We captured and brought back to camp five Jap sailors. We got a Jap canteen, machete, pocket knives, Jap paper money and coins. When we first encountered them, they resisted but we finally persuaded them with a hand grenade. We saw a 5" dud shell, which exploded after we were about 500 yards from it. During the night we were shelled by a Jap submarine. Jap troop ships were on their way but the Navy ships and planes drove them off. When we went back in the afternoon, we had to come back as we encountered too many Japs.

Monday, August 24, 1942

About 2:30 P.M. we had an air raid by Jap planes; six bombers and 11 Zero fighters. They dropped 19 bombs but only two went off. The six bombers never left the island before they were downed. We lost three planes. One was shot down by the Marines. Drew some more Jap supplies. Issued us Jap cigarettes and cookies. Went over to the top sergeant and drew some matches and Jap socks. Around midnight we had an awful shelling from a Jap cruiser and believe me the shells were really flying around us. I thought the whole Jap fleet must have been out there. Tomorrow we start coffee and hard-tack for breakfast and supper.

Tuesday, August 25, 1942

Davis and I went down to where the battle was fought. We lost 32 men and had 68 wounded. There were over 1,000 dead Japs. We went over to the airport and saw our planes. Five bombers and six Cobras. Then we had a terrific air raid. Twenty-one Jap bombers flew over and bombed us. Picked up a Jap flag on the battlefield and it's really shot up. Tomorrow we're going to move the galley across the road. Also we lost one plane.

Wednesday, August 26, 1942

Sure was a tough day. I got the shits. My stomach is cramped up pretty bad and a headache and a fever. Around dinner time we had another raid from the Japs. Got the news today that I made corporal in line of duty. Hoff, Davis, Collins, and Ted also made it. That made me feel a little better. We got eight Jap bombers today and five Jap Zero fighters.

Thursday, August 27, 1942

Nothing much going on today. We had an air raid warning today. We got some ship in that sea battle Monday. Just got it over the radio; it's been confirmed; two transports, two cruisers, two destroyers, one battleship, one aircraft carrier. Also knocked down four Zero fighters. Mosquito bites. I'm covered with them. It looks like I got a rash all over my body but it's just mosquito bites and the flies are terrible from dawn till dark. Collins made sergeant.

Friday, August 28, 1942

Up until yesterday, we've got 69 planes. Weather is still very hot and mosquitoes are still very bad. Going to set up a bakery and Tebbe is going to be a baker again. We've got the oven and have it all set up. Each man got a small ration of fresh bread. First piece of bread we have had since we landed. No air raid for a change. Think they must have a day off today. Went swimming in the river in the evening. I hate war. Again, again, again, again I say I hate war. Field stripped my rifle and bayonet today for the first time and it sure did need it.

Saturday, August 29, 1942

Had two air raids today; one early in the morning around 5:00 A.M. and the other one now at 12 noon. That's when they started it. Now 12:30 and things are still going strong. Our anti-aircraft guns just knocked down two Jap airplanes. We made doughnuts this morning and boy, they really are good. Best I ever tasted. Sounds like all hell is breaking loose around here. Rifle shots are popping and half tracks now. Don't know what's going on now. Went up the beach to the harbor and saw the Jap village we took last week and saw the ships. There were two destroyers and three cargo ships. Hoff, Collins, and Davis made chief cook. Saw one of the Jap planes come down and crash. Made some biscuits which were pretty good.

Sunday, August 30, 1942

Lost one destroyer today: the *Calhoun*. It was sunk by a Jap bomber. It sunk in less than three minutes after it was hit. Lost quite a few men on it. They didn't have a chance to get off. We sunk one Jap submarine. Another air raid again today. We got some fresh meat today. First since being on the island. We got some pork loin and two halves of veal. The fellows nearly went crazy trying to get some. Had biscuits again today. Still feeling pretty bad. An awful lot of the fellows are getting sick so I am not by myself. Wrote a letter to Ruth today and washed a few clothes.

Monday, August 31, 1942

Andy Rosko's birthday today; he's 24 years old. Hell of a place to have a birthday. Had another air raid again today. It's getting to be pretty monotonous. Lot of men from the Raider Battalion came over here from Tulagi. Talked to some colored Fiji Island Police that were on the *Calhoun* and got off alright. As yet we still haven't had any mail since leaving the States. Found a Jap flower bush and the smell of the buds is wonderful; so sweet. Never smelled anything like it before in my life. Going to press it and take it back to the States. Having a real treat tonight. Fresh meat; veal stew and fresh-baked biscuits.

Tuesday, September 1, 1942

Had an air raid again today. Six Zero fighters were brought down. We lost three planes today. Saw a torpedo today on the beach. Biggest one I ever saw; over 25 feet long. Around 3:00 A.M. Wednesday morning we had a bombing. It's getting so you can't even sleep any more. They can't be union fighters as they bomb us 24 hours a day or night. Shipped out over 400 Jap prisoners yesterday. Also mail came in. I didn't get any yet but expect to. It's rumored that quite a few Jap troops landed on the island. Davis got transferred into C Company.

Wednesday, September 2, 1942

Well this is one day I know I will never forget. The Jap planes came over today and gave us a real bombing. They dropped 18 bombs. Two hit near by me. The concussion knocked me on the ground. I got my neck and arm cut by shrapnel but not serious. The fellows keep telling me I'm the luckiest one in the battalion. Also received mail today. First mail I have received since leaving the States. Received two letters from the folks dated July 11th and 15th. One from Jeanne dated July 10th. The Japs landed 20 miles up the beach. Our outfit is standing by as we're going to attack tomorrow. The troops are moving up now. Also dug a shelter after that bombing today. That was just a little too close for comfort.

Thursday, September 3, 1942

Still feeling pretty bad in my stomach. Had a half bottle of Jap beer today. Hear we're leaving pretty soon. Will probably go back to New Zealand or Australia for reorganization. Heard the news broadcast from the States and also some music. Boy, it sure did sound good. Captain Edwards left us as he is pretty sick but will rejoin us wherever we reorganize. The Army is supposed to start moving in tomorrow. Up until August 31st, the planes with us have destroyed 16 twin-engine bombers, five single-engine bombers, 39 Zeros and three destroyers and they have hit and probably destroyed one cruiser and two destroyers and two transports.

Friday, September 4, 1942

Raining all day long. I guess it's just about time for the rainy season to start down here. Japs bombed us again today. They don't like to let us rest. I'm still not feeling so good. The Japs are supposed to be about 18 miles down the beach from us. I wrote to Reta, Mother, Jeanne, and Eileen today. Some more ships are in and the trucks are hauling supplies in a steady stream. We got some fresh beef today. Talked to the captain of the Parachutes. He said they buried 970 Japs, lost 32, and 84 wounded; 305 active men left. They underestimated the Japs. They only figured on 400 Japs there. Worked on our bomb shelter today.

Saturday, September 5, 1942

Early this morning we had a real shelling, complements of Tojo. Had a little naval battle; some Jap cruisers come in and they sunk three of our A.P.D.s. (American Patrol Destroyers). In the afternoon we had an air raid but the bombs didn't do any damage as they dropped them in the hills. Eighteen bombers and 26 Zeros came over. We didn't lose any planes at all. We got three bombers and five Zero fighters. Saw a bunch of wounded sailors from the A.P.D. that got sunk. Three men came back in our outfit from H & S Companies; they were in New Caledonia and came over here on the *Fomalhaut*.

Sunday, September 6, 1942

Got some fresh beef today; two hindquarters and a forequarter. Steak tonight for supper and stew for breakfast and it's all gone. Had some palm cabbage for supper. Rained nearly all day long. The other night when we were getting shelled, a fellow was singing, "I don't want a BAR, all I want is Hedy Lamarr." The Raiders moved out today. We got 35 planes yesterday. The Lexington got 24 planes and we got three here.

Monday, September 7, 1942

Weather is still damp and raining. Boy, this sure is a mud-hole when it rains. No shelling or bombing for over 24 hours. Seems funny to have such a quiet day. Went over to the airport; saw five planes that were smashed up. Only one got hurt during the bombing. We got two twin-motored planes in. Teddy bought a sheath knife for $10.00. Everything pretty quiet in general. Heard they shot one man over at the airport for sleeping at his post. Labor Day today but you would never know it. Feeling a little better.

Tuesday, September 8, 1942

Went down to the beach. The Raiders and the Parachuters left. Saw them pull out. Two ships came in; the *Fuller* and the *Bellatrix*. Saw two truckloads of mail come off the ships. Stopped going to the doctor today. Had a bombing tonight at 7:00 P.M. We lost six planes that cracked up on account of the muddy wet weather which made the runway so slippery. That Marine they shot at the airport caused four men to lose their lives. Around midnight, had a shelling from the Japs.

Wednesday, September 9, 1942

One of the nicest fellows in our outfit died today at the hospital. Joe Carly. Sure did hate to see him go. Got mail today. Received one letter. It was from Margarita in North Carolina. Davis went to the hospital to be treated today. Got two more stoves and cabinets today. Starting tomorrow, we go on three meals a day. They fixed up the Jap power plant and made connections to the airport so now we have our own electricity for our airport.

Thursday, September 10, 1942

Japs tried to break through last night right behind us but were driven off by the 2nd and 5th Marine Battalions. At 12 noon today, we had an air raid; 30 Jap planes came over and bombed us. Saw two Jap planes get shot down right above us by our planes. Cleaned rising gun, packed it in grease, and packed it away. Outside of the one bombing we had today, things were pretty quiet. Wrote a letter to Mother and Margarita and sent them a picture of me in blues. Joe's grave made the 71st one. Today 16 more men joined him; they were killed by the bombs. Personnel bombs designed to kill men on the ground. They had glass, razor blades, iron, chain links, etc. More mail came today; we'll probably get it tomorrow or the next day.

Friday, September 11, 1942

Had another air raid today; one early in the morning and one in the afternoon. We got 13 Zero fighters and three bombers. Half our outfit moved up about five miles and are forming a first defense line. Also, late in the afternoon we got some more plane reinforcements as during the raids, we only had 12 fighters that could get off the ground. 22 planes and eight Flying Fortresses. The Fortresses are taking off tomorrow morning on air raid.

Saturday, September 12, 1942

Our men moved out to the hills and I went up with them. The air raid came and I really saw a beautiful sight. Was up in the hills behind the airport when a couple of bombs came pretty close to us. Our anti-aircraft knocked down five Jap bombers, two of them fell within two blocks of us, and our planes got 11 bombers and three Zero fighters. In the hills it is really hot and no protection of any kind; just bare hills. They had high grass on them but we burnt it all off. Got a piece of Jap bomber and a small piece of one of the parachutes. One of the bombers got nearly to the ground and then it blew up and small pieces were floating down for over twenty minutes. The leg of one of the Jap pilots landed not very far from us. In the one bomber, we found the bones of two Jap pilots. Lost one man in the million-dollar radio shack; a direct hit by the Jap bombs.

Sunday, September 13, 1942

Had two good shellings last night by the Japs. Started around 10:00 P.M. and lasted until 10:45 P.M. and another around 11:30 P.M. They dropped flares and shone searchlights which lighted up our area. At 5:30 A.M. we had a bombing; it was just at dawn and then around 9:00 A.M. we had our second bombing. I saw three airplanes go down and one pilot bail out but a plane dove down on him and opened up his machine gun on him. 1:30 P.M. third bombing so far today. I guess Tojo is trying to crack my nerves; he's going to get fooled. Quite a few fellows are cracking up; it's too much on their nerves. Pretty soon, I'll go to get Japs myself. Can't even get a decent night's sleep. Around 5:00 P.M. had another attack. Two Jap airplanes broke through and nobody knew anything about it until they shot down one of our planes coming into land and started strafing our whole camp with machine gun bullets and I hit the deck in a hurry.

Monday, September 14, 1942

The Japs attacked last night and we were up all night long. They broke through and got three of our 20 MM guns and forced back the Raiders and Parachutes. We got 36 Jap planes yesterday. Four Zeros today. Had an air raid at 10:00 A.M. Japs tried to form a pincher movement on us. Two fellows went out of their heads yesterday in camp during an air raid. Our plane that was shot down landed in our camp about 1,000 yards from where we were. Had another air raid around 2:00 P.M. and about 5:30 P.M. some Jap seaplanes broke through and dropped some personnel bombs and strafed our whole camp. Boy, I really did travel when that machine gun's bullets hit the ground. Fifteen Jap planes came in and six left; we got the other nine. Boy, the fireworks have really been going. Raiders pushed back the Japs. One fellow shot himself in the foot during an air raid.

Tuesday, September 15, 1942

We had three air raids today and gunfire was very heavy all day long. The Japs have been forced back and Roy shot one sniper. Yesterday 2,165 dead Japs were counted and buried. H & S of our outfit went out looking for snipers and also got one. Some Marines came off of the island behind Tulagi. We fed 250 of them. Had to buy a carton of cigarettes; first ones I bought since leaving the ship. Have a Navy task force out at sea nearby to stay out there as long as we're on the island. The 7th Marines are supposed to come in tomorrow morning. Davis came back from the hospital. Going up into the hills tomorrow and see if I can find some excitement. No strafing or shelling in our camp for a whole day.

Wednesday, September 16, 1942

Had machine gun fire and rifle fire all night long but the Japs didn't get through to us. Morning started out by raining. In the afternoon we went up into the hills with the chow. Had an air raid while we were there. Hotter than the devil up there. I really got burnt. The wind is quite bad up there; blows the dust so bad you can't see two feet in front of you. Heard we lost two fellows in the Tank Corps that I got to know pretty well. Sergeant Brownson and Schwartz. Saw one of the fellows bring a white parrot into camp today.

He caught it and tamed it. The score in the last couple of days is 2,400 Japs dead on the island. One fellow was sick and didn't have half his gear but he still kept the parrot.

Thursday, September 17, 1942

I sent home two letters yesterday to Mother and Dad. No air raids all day long. Went up in the hills again. Boy, it sure is rugged country up there. So far we got 175 Jap airplanes. That's both Zeros and bombers. Marines are holding out and were still fighting. Pretty quiet day, just a little machine gun fire. Killed 1,500 Japs down on the beach when the Japs tried to land and form a beachhead. Collins bought a Jap watch; he paid $50.00 for it. Had a big sea battle; we got six Jap ships. Our planes bombing the ships all day long. The 7th Marines are supposed to come in tomorrow along with 15 ships. In the hills, you can see smoke coming up from Jap camps and occasional shots are fired by Jap snipers.

Friday, September 18, 1942

Seventh Marines came in and landed today. Parachutes and Raiders left there going back to the States. They said mail came in today too. Five thousand Marines came in all total. Six cargo ships came in hauling ammunition and supplies all day long. Got hold of some Stateside peanuts. Ten tractors came in today from New Hebrides. Got hold of a new steak knife today. Pretty quiet all day long; not much firing of any kind. No air raid or shelling all day long.

Saturday, September 19, 1942

Had some shelling last night. Four boys from the 7th got killed and four were wounded. Received a letter from Reta in New Zealand. Some other outfit is taking over the defense line in the hills and our boys are forming a beach defense. Raiders are going out on another raid. No air raids again today. A little too quiet to suit me. I guess in a few days everything will break loose again. Got a carton of smokes, jacket, and socks from Roy. Saw a bunch of fellows from the 7th and the 11th go by us yesterday. We sure kidded them and told them they would act a lot different after they had been under fire.

Sunday, September 20, 1942

Around 8:00 A.M. things started popping. The big guns let loose, trench mortars, 155s, etc. Sure is pretty noisy. 10:00 A.M. had an air raid. Our Flying Fortress is named "Bessie the Jap Basher." Raiders came back from the hills. Heavy artillery firing all night long. Heard the 7th killed quite a few of their own men; accidentally thinking they were Japs. Went out to the beach with the chow. Going out for supper through the jungle, some Jap snipers fired on us but didn't hit us luckily. Saw some Jap field pieces and pill boxes they evacuated and which we are now defending. Went over to the airport in the evening and I was looking over our torpedo bombers.

Monday, September 21, 1942

Part of our outfit came back. Eighteen of them which had been over on Tulagi. Like old home week. Saw one fellow get smashed up a little bit; he got caught between a truck and a tree. Got some cigarettes today; stateside stuff. Raiders went out on a raid; they killed 180 Japs. Raiders had no casualties. Ships supposed to come in tomorrow with mail, etc. One fellow got a bayonet in him twice because he didn't answer when challenged. Tebbe saw and shot a wild boar.

SHIPS IN ORDER FOR LANDING FORCE!

Hunter Liggett P-27
Alchiba K-23
Fomalhaut K-22
Betelgeuse K-28
Crescent City P-40
President Hayes P-39
President Adams P-38
Alhena K-26
Heywood P-12
Fuller P-14
American Legion P-35
Bellatrix K-20
McCawley P-10
Barnett P-11
GF Elliott P-13
Libra K-53

Tuesday, September 22, 1942

No bombing or shellings. One of our few quiet days. Got a good supply of cigarettes in the company office. Drew some new clothes as everybody needed them badly. We received five new Air Cobras. Hoff got a pistol he found. We should have superiority in the air now.

Wednesday, September 23, 1942

Sergeant Small went to the hospital and nearly 1/3 of my company is laid up on account of sickness. Walter Winchell says we'll be back in the States by

Christmas. Had pie today. First time since before we left New Zealand. Galley force was increased today. Got three new strikers for cook. First night I slept undisturbed since being on the island. Hope of mail coming in tomorrow.

Thursday, September 24, 1942

Ship came in today; it was the *Betelgeuse* K-28. I went aboard with Davis and Hoff; couldn't buy anything. We finally bought apples for a dollar. We finally got some PX supplies in camp today. I bought some toothpaste, razor blades, candy bar, and a package of gum, a towel and some writing paper. Davis owes me 60 cents and Tebbe owes me 40 cents. Loaned Clark $2.00; promised to give me back $4.00 payday.

Saturday, September 26, 1942

Got a pair of Jap gloves today and a U.S. sweater. Wrote a letter to George Moore and Uncle Jack. Raining off and on all day long. One of our sergeants left for New Caledonia to take an exam for Marine gunner. Guns firing again today. Played the Marine Hymn for the 1st Marine Division in the Solomon Islands. (That's us.) Two ships in; the *Betelgeuse* and the *Helena*.

Sunday, September 27, 1942

Saw ten Flying Fortresses come in yesterday. Also we caught a live calf which we are keeping here. Boy, we sure had a rotten time today. At 12:50 P.M. an air raid started; they came from two directions. Seventeen bombers in all plus Zero fighters which escorted them. Lindsey got killed. Batten was seriously wounded. They were about 30 yards from me. Two bombs dropped within 30 yards of me. Shrapnel was flying all over. I was covered with dirt. Fifteen bombs were dropped in our camp area. In the raid, we lost seven men and 25 were wounded but we got approximately 250 to 300 Japs. Firing all day long; trench mortars, 75s, machine guns, bombs, anti-aircraft guns. Don't want to see any more days like this.

Tuesday, September 29, 1942

Had another air raid again today around 1:30 P.M. In the last week we've got four Jap ships and 33 airplanes. So far we've got 36 Jap ships, 31 of which have been warships and a total of 209 planes of various types. Lost one Flying Fortress over Bouganville. We shot down four Zeros and lost one. Also we got seven more planes in. Have 2,000 Japs trapped in the hills of which 500 are sick and wounded. Our Fortress bombed at 6,000 feet. Our big guns are continuously firing all day long. During the night we send up flares. Things are sure getting noisy and hot around here, again.

Wednesday, September 30, 1942

Uneventful; no bombings or shelling. Rained continuously all day long. Big guns still firing all day long. Our young bull is getting to be quite a pet. One of the fellows has a baby wild boar for a pet. Wrote a letter to Roy Mock's sister. Mail is supposed to come tomorrow.

Thursday, October 1, 1942

Ship didn't come in today. Expecting an attack either tonight or tomorrow. Captain Fuller and Captain Manefield left at 5:30 A.M. by plane for the States to start training men for a 3rd Division. One general came in today and decorated some aviators and some of the Raiders for bravery and outstanding accomplishments. Tebbe paid me back $2.00 he owed me. At 8:30 P.M. a Jap plane came over and dropped a few bombs and boy, we sure did scatter.

Friday, October 2, 1942

At 4:15 A.M., two more planes came over and dropped some bombs; a couple landed in our area and dirt flew all over our tent. Two ships came in today. At 12:45 P.M. we had another air raid. Before the raid, I went over to the airport and brought back a piece of Zero plane, a few small pieces of the wing. A few Japs landed last night. Our planes were strafing them all day. Mail comes in today.

Saturday, October 3, 1942

Had one air raid today about 12:30 P.M. and boy, they sure came close. One Jap plane came down and strafed the ground. They hit all around my foxhole. Around 11:00 P.M. that lone Jap plane came in again and dropped bombs. We were on the alert all night. Reported four destroyers and one cruiser on the way expected at around 11:00 P.M.

Sunday, October 4, 1942

Last night our planes got one cruiser and one destroyer. Boy, it sure is hotter than the devil today. Wrote to Mother, Myron, Mike, and Jeanne. Traded some Jap stuff for some candy with the pilot at the airport. Beautiful day for an air raid.

Monday, October 5, 1942

That lone Jap plane got in again around 3:00 A.M.; dropped a bomb and beat it. Boy, it sure is hot again today. We got nine more of our boys in that didn't get off the ship August 7th. Also our greens came in. Our young bull is getting to be quite a pet. He follows Andy around like a dog. The fellows put him in a shelter hole when we have an air raid. Saw two wild chickens. They are pretty. Half blue and half black and white tail.

Tuesday, October 6, 1942

Boy, I sure was sick last night; don't feel any too hot now. Had our pictures taken by aviation photographers. Said our planes sunk two Jap destroyers last night. Also, the Japs landed some reinforcements. Wrote a couple of letters home. Firing still continues day and night.

Wednesday, October 7, 1942

We finally got our pictures and boy, they really turned out swell. Giving the Japs in the hills hell. Our dive-bombers sunk a Jap cruiser off the coast of Guadalcanal, which makes 29 Jap warships sunk in the Solomon area. Got some more planes in. An alert all night long; five Jap ships headed this way; expected around 11:00 P.M.

Thursday, October 8, 1942

We went up to the front lines today and boy, it sure was hot up there. A couple of Jap snipers had us pinned down so we couldn't move. Saw bananas, pineapples, and figs. Also saw dead Japs and Marines. Saw a small two-mast schooner which was sunk close to shore and also the Japs landing boats which were hidden along the shore. Jap plane came in and bombed us after maneuvering around overhead for about 45 minutes.

Friday, October 9, 1942

Over the radio, it said that we got one heavy cruiser, two destroyers, one airplane tender, two transports, two cargo vessels, and 22 airplanes. Collins got a Jap bayonet. Heard the Army is going to come in tomorrow. Still fighting on the island. Gunfire and air raids still keep us going. Had an air raid around 12:30 P.M. and had another around 4:00 P.M. but our planes took care of them. Heavy artillery still continues to fire day and night.

Saturday, October 10, 1942

Rosko and I went up to the front lines this morning and crossed the river with K Company. After we crossed the river, our planes bombed and strafed us. I hit the deck and prayed. Brought back a Jap gas mask and club. Tebbe got a Jap bayonet. Army supposed to come in the 13th and the Raiders are to go back home. Boy, that one day, it was sure hot. We got three Jap cruisers today.

Sunday, October 11, 1942

We had an air raid that lasted for one and a half hours. We got 11 bombers and four Zeros. Jap ships coming in to try and get us. Bernie made corporal today. Four Jap cruisers and four Jap destroyers are coming in but our ships are waiting for them. Made a drawing on Jap signal flag.

Monday, October 12, 1942

We had a sea battle last night. We got all eight of the Jap ships. Six were sunk and the other two were damaged. We sent our planes out to finish them off this morning. So far we've sunk 75 Jap ships. We lost 36 men dead, and over 200 wounded up at the front in the hills.

Tuesday, October 13, 1942

Well, it's my birthday today. I am 23 years old today. The Army came in this morning and 30 of our men from New Caledonia. Had an air raid around 10:00 A.M. and had our second air raid around 1:30 P.M. In the evening, the Japs started shelling us with artillery from the hills. Then three Jap ships came in and shelled us and planes dropped flares and bombed us. I moved out with the company and set up a defense in case they tried to cross the river. I really was scared.

Wednesday, October 14, 1942

Up all night long. They didn't stop bombing us until dawn. Had an air raid today around 10:00 P.M. and had another air raid around 1:30 P.M. First wave there was around 40 planes, and the second wave around eight planes. Had another air raid around 5:00 P.M. It seems all I can hear is bombs dropping and planes coming over. The little sleep I do get, I dream of being bombed. In the evening they shelled us from the sea, planes bombed us from the skies and artillery shelled us from the hills.

Thursday, October 15, 1942

First thing the morning we saw 18 Jap ships out in the bay. Six of them were transports and we could see them unloading men and stuff in their landing boats. Our planes couldn't get through their anti-aircraft fire. Our Flying Fortresses came over and sunk three Jap transports. Had five air raids. One Jap Zero came over and strafed us and boy, I sure hit the deck. But our planes brought him down. In the evening, Hill Billy Joe was firing at us. Sent 20 tanks up after him. Louie the Louse came over and dropped bombs and flares and one landed about 30 yards from us. Came over later and dropped six more. Three Jap transports were burning and went down in late evening. One made nine explosions before it went down.

Friday, October 16, 1942

Had one air raid around 8:45 A.M. to start the day off with. So far it is said we got 18 Jap ships in the last 24 hours and seven which just came over the radio. One of which was a Jap warship. So far we've got 293 Jap planes and 63 ships in the area. Had an air raid around 10:30 A.M. and had another around 1:30 P.M. and one late in the afternoon. Waiting for Louie but he didn't come over. Japs sunk one of our inter-island ships but our planes got all six dive bombers.

Saturday, October 17, 1942

Had an air raid around 9:00 A.M. and then we had another 10:00 A.M. Then in the afternoon we had another one which dropped 100 yards away and exploded mortar shells and drums of oil. There was an immense fire which burned for around three to four hours. We lost one man. Boy, if this keeps up all the men will go screwy. Also got a couple of pictures from my friend. Saw our anti-aircraft guns bring down three Jap planes.

Sunday, October 18, 1942

Had an air raid around 12:30 P.M. They didn't drop any bombs in our area but they dropped personnels and I saw them bring in ten men. Around midnight last night a Jap destroyer came in and really gave us a shelling. Two duds landed up at the head 100 yards away. One over at sick bay. One landed in a hole with eight of our boys but didn't go off but it caved it in and shook them up quite a bit. So far we've spent 72 days on this island.

Monday, October 19, 1942

Had two air raids; one around 10:00 A.M. and one in the afternoon but neither one of them got through. Yesterday our planes got 13 bombers and nine Zeros. Also yesterday we lost five men and 31 wounded by the bombs, which got a direct hit on the Division PX. Hoff, Davis, and Collins all went to the hospital with malaria. Moved out to the beach. Seventy Japs broke through but the Army got them. Might get a shelling; four Jap cruisers and four destroyers are headed this way.

Tuesday, October 20, 1942

Out at the beach now. Went into the main camp. Had two air raids. Hill Billy Joe fired at us but it hit the water a good 200 yards away. Neither time did the Jap planes get through. In the evening right after dark, two Jap planes sneaked in and dropped about six bombs. One landed 25 feet from us in the road. Had search lights on them and the anti-aircraft opened up. They came back twice after that so we didn't get to sleep until after midnight.

Wednesday, October 21, 1942

Had an air raid today. Seven of them got over and they killed nine men and had 81 casualties. Hill Billy Joe is still firing down in this area. Last night around dark, one hit about 100 yards away in the water. Louie the Louse and his brother came over and dropped eight bombs in our area; they were all personnels. Four landed within 100 yards of us and threw stuff all over us. Had no casualties. The second time over he didn't bomb our area. Also sent a letter home to the folks.

Thursday, October 22, 1942

Had a couple of air raids today but none of them got through in the afternoon. In the morning they did get in and dive bomb on one of the ships that was unloading but they didn't get it. We got six Jap dive bombers and lost none. Hill Billy Joe is still firing at us. Louie the Louse didn't come in last night. All evening long was very quiet.

Friday, October 23, 1942

Had an air raid today about 11:00 A.M. They didn't get to do any damage. I saw five Jap planes get shot down in smoke. Those dogfights sure were nice to see. Then the Japs tried to break through on our west flank late in the evening and all night long all hell broke loose. Shells were flying over us; some going and some coming.

Saturday, October 24, 1942

No air raid today. Hill Billy Joe is still throwing shells down here. A few of them landed too close for comfort. Started raining and of course that didn't make things very comfortable. Back in the hills, the battle still goes on. They were supposed to have killed 2,000 Japs and captured some Jap tanks. I got a book, *Harbor Nights,* and read it and made a signal flag for my buddy Valincourt.

Sunday, October 25, 1942

Well, today makes 79 days on the island. Eleven Jap Zeros came over today around 8:00 A.M. We thought they were ours but we found out different. Boy, we sure had a ringside seat today. Five Jap ships came in and started shelling around 9:30 A.M.; they set fire and sunk our two inner-island boats they were dog-fighting overhead. I saw five planes go down in smoke. In two planes the pilots bailed out and our Higgins boats went out to get them. Later on another raid, and dog-fights galore above us. Score; lost one plane, pilot saved. Japs lost 26 planes; three ships and five tanks on land.

Monday, October 26, 1942

Pretty quiet today. No air raids as yet and it's now 3:00 P.M. Heavy artillery firing all night, both ours and the Japs. The Japs tried to break through again last night by the 1st Marines. They killed over 1,000 Japs. Our Fortresses bombed the Japs in the hills with blockbusters; lightest one weighed 1,000 pounds. I cut my hand pretty bad and they wanted to stitch it but I wouldn't let them. Got a Testament from Aurora Church. We blew up two of our tractors today just before dark when our planes were coming in, one went into a barrel roll and crashed in the lagoon in C Company area.

Tuesday, October 27, 1942

Summer is now setting in on the tropics. It sure is getting hot. I'm getting my fill of the tropics. This is the only place where the lightening bugs drop flares and the mosquitoes dive on you. Still firing all night. The Japs have attacked us from B side all except the last side which is the sea and expecting an attack momentarily.

Wednesday, October 28, 1942

Started for the front yesterday but didn't get all the way up as they stopped us, not having helmets or arms. Oscar and his brother came over and dropped his bombs pretty close. Foster got busted. Jap submarine reported in the vicinity; it got through our Navy. Also heard that reinforcements are coming and we are to leave the island very shortly. More information to be received later. Some mail came in but I didn't receive any. Admiral Halsey is now in command of the Navy. Nimitz has been relieved.

Thursday, October 29, 1942

Nothing happened today of any importance. Our planes dropped bombs on the Japs in the hills. I just hope that they are doing some damage up there. Nothing going on in the air or on the sea. Of course they are still fighting up in the hills.

Friday, October 30, 1942

Went up to the front lines today and got a Jap bayonet. We walked nearly 10 miles to get up to the front through jungles and into the hills. Got caught in a rainstorm coming back. Then we had two rivers to cross. On the first, Mac, Hanna, and myself nearly drowned. Hanna went under and finally got across but lost his rifle, cartridge belt, bayonet, and canteen. Mac and I left our rifles the other side of the river and finally got back to camp around 8:30 P.M.

Saturday, October 31, 1942

Mac and I finally got our rifles; they were still there but in terrible shape. I had to detail strip my rifle. Things are pretty quiet in general today. A new order put out no swimming in the ocean on account of the great number of sharks now in these waters. Hill Billy Joe is back at it again today. One landed right by our area, only out in the water. Our planes bombed the Japs in the hills today.

Sunday, November 1, 1942

For a Sunday, this is the quietest one we have had since landing on the island. No air raids at all. But they are really going after the Japs in the hills. Today they moved the artillery up a few more miles and have started a drive to wipe out the Japs up there. Some ships are supposed to come in tomorrow and I hope some relief comes in with them. Weather is getting awful hot down here now and I still do not think I'll be home for Christmas.

Monday, November 2, 1942

Went up to the front lines today and it sure was plenty hot. Helped take ammunition up to the front lines; just got it unloaded and the Japs opened up on us. Helped load eight wounded men on the truck under fire. They sure had me scared for a while. Five destroyers and three cargo ships came in. Also some Marines from the 2nd Regiment came in. They just came back from a raid 52 miles down the coast. Also got 155 MM guns in today.

Tuesday, November 3, 1942

Yesterday at the front, eight Jap tanks were captured and blown up. Artillery firing up in the hills using our new 155 MM guns. Marines are still pushing the Japs back. The main part of the Japs are pretty well scattered. Ships are back in again today and are unloading a lot of stuff. Our planes are now bombing the Japs at the lower end of the island.

Wednesday, November 4, 1942

Ships came in with more troops; the 6th, 8th, and 10th Marines all came in. The 10th is artillery like the 11th. We had three ships and 13 warships, a couple of cruisers and the rest destroyers. The *Barnett, Alchiba*, *Hunter*, and *H. Liggett.* They shelled the Japs at both ends of the island. November 2nd, the Japs landed 1,200 more men and 17 ships were headed this way. Five got through. One battalion ambushed them and another went down yesterday plus shelling and artillery; they figure only about 200 left. Still advancing at the upper end of the island. One Jap battleship got four hits on it. Also sunk one cruiser and one other Jap warship.

Thursday, November 5, 1942

Ships came back in again today. We finally had an air raid today. Just like old times. I saw three go down from anti-aircraft fire. Wrote a letter home to the folks. One of our boys got a piece of shrapnel in his arm. Brooks in H 7 5 has been missing for three days now. Fighting still continues in the hills and down at the other end of the island.

Friday, November 6, 1942

Christy found a Jap sleeping in his tractor and shot him with a Lewis gun right through the cab. I got some mahogany wood; they make fence posts out of it and we use it for firewood. Went down to the beach; the natives, around 500 of them, were unloading the Higgins boats. I traded my shirt to a native for a Chinese belt made in Hong Kong. He got it off a Jap. Last night, Louie the Louse came over and dropped a couple of flares and a few bombs but they didn't hit in our area. We got some real potatoes in today. What a treat!

Saturday, November 7, 1942

Well, the day started out by raining. Then along around 8:00 A.M. loud naval gunfire could be heard. A Jap sub fired one torpedo and got a hit on one of our ships. Then the destroyers started throwing depth charges which shook the ground under foot. A few hours later, oil could be seen all over; it washed up on the beach. Now the beach is covered with oil for miles and the sea. We saw eight sharks a little ways out. They said we got the sub and that was probably the reason for the appearance of the sharks. Our company was notified to be packed by the 20th of November. Eleven Jap ships are reported to be coming in tonight.

Sunday, November 8, 1942

Last night our planes got four Jap warships which they sunk and made hits on six other Jap ships at the cost of four of our planes and one pilot. Raining again today. Heard we're supposed to get two candy bars apiece tonight. Got Mac's flag about ¾ done. Got two candy bars, a box of crackers, cigarettes, and matches. Life goes on just the same. We now have over 500 Marines buried in our graveyard over here. Saw one of our Douglas Transports crash; all perished. Crew of three and 18 men which were wounded and being evacuated. Our PT boat got a Jap ship in the searchlight and let go with torpedoes and .50 caliber tracer slugs. A beautiful sight.

Monday, November 9, 1942

We were issued some new clothing today if you had the old clothing to turn in to be surveyed. Mr. Nooman shot a Jap that was using a hand machine gun up on the front lines. Heard today that we go to White Poppy from here. Got lit on some homemade stuff and it really is potent. Also we are going to receive no more mail over here. We will get it at our next destination. Recipe; one-gallon jug, about two inches raisins, little yeast, ¾ full of water and sugar. Let set and add sugar daily for about five days.

Tuesday, November 10, 1942

Well, this now makes 95 days on the island. Had an air raid this morning around 10:15 A.M. but none of them got through. They got within ten miles and our planes took out after them. Last report I heard, they were 70 miles from the island and still going. Today is the Marine Anniversary; started in 1775, November 10th. Also 12 Air Cobras took off with our fighters to intercept the 12 Jap Zeros. Have a mine sweeper out here. Now we're expecting some ships in tomorrow. Also the 5th Marines are supposed to leave tomorrow.

Wednesday, November 11, 1942

Around 9:00 A.M. we had an air raid. I saw seven out of 12 Jap planes go down in smoke. Also saw one of our planes crash about 800 yards out in the ocean. He bailed out and the Higgins boat picked him up. Eight of our ships came in this morning. Had another air raid around 12:30 P.M. I counted 24 bombers that flew over us. We got five that I saw go down and maybe more. I received a box of stationary from Eileen and mail from Mike, Eileen, Tom, his wife, Jeanne, folks, and Neil.

Thursday, November 12, 1942

Well, we had an air raid around 9:00 A.M. and one around 2:00 P.M. Our ships came in today bringing one Army Division, six transports and cargo ships, and 18 warships. The Japs came in. Around 20 or more with twin-motored jobs flying just around 20 or 30 yards above the surface. Boy, our whole fleet started blasting them and it sure didn't last very long. They made short work of the Japs. We got 16 Jap bombers and five Jap Zeros.

Friday, November 13, 1942

Well, we really had quite a day today. The sea battle is supposed to be going on and more fighting than last night. Around 10:30 P.M. they really started battling last night. You could see star shells, flares, tracers. Ships exploding and burning, big searchlights, etc. We could see Higgins boats bringing in survivors and sharks were seen 30 yards off shore. We also got in some Lockheed Interceptors; eight altogether. We got nine Jap planes and lost one. On the sea, we sunk two Jap battleships and seriously damaged one. Numerous destroyers. We lost the *Atlanta* and two destroyers and two or three other ships were damaged. We have one survivor off the *Atlanta* in our camp now. In the afternoon, a big Jap bomber sneaked in on us and strafed us.

Saturday, November 14, 1942

Early this morning, around 2:30 A.M., a Jap battleship and two other warships started shelling us. They shelled us for about one hour. Boy, they sounded like freight trains going over our heads. They came in to rescue three damaged battleships. They are towing it back and our planes are out after them. We had two air raids today. One around 8:00 A.M. and another around 10:30 A.M. Pay master is here today and we can draw up to $25.00. The last three days and nights it really has been hot around here. We are getting ready for an invasion and landing party on the beach tonight at dusk. That's about 1 ½ hours from now. Twenty-five Jap transports are coming in with warships escorting them.

Sunday, November 15, 1942

Well, our planes split them up in two groups last night. In the combat group, we sank three light cruisers and one destroyer. In the AP group, three were sunk and three were damaged so that they couldn't move. Two were burning, and the other four dragged anchor and one of these had a hit on it. Early this morning some Jap ships could be seen unloading. Our planes set three of these on fire. Today is 100 days on the island. Late last night there was a big naval battle but we received no confirmed news on it. We received word just now that three Jap battleships were sunk in the naval battle. Some mail came in and packages. I received a V-mail from Mother.

Monday, November 16, 1942

So far nothing of any importance has happened. The Jap ships are still burning out there. Artillery is still continuing to fire with the Japs throwing a few shells down here. Every once in a while, a close one startles you. It's been raining all day long and still raining. So far no air raids at all. Heard some more Army coming in pretty soon. We got 18 Jap bombers and fighters and lost seven of ours. New planes coming in all the time. Interceptors, Fortresses, twin-motored bombers, dive bombers, torpedo bombers, and fighters.

Tuesday, November 17, 1942

Nothing happened today. No air raids or anything! It's too quiet and monotonous with no shellings or bombing or air raids or sea battles. Heard that the four Jap APs that got away from here with one hit, were sunk up the coast a ways. Also they sunk two more transports up on New Guinea. Of course, the fighting still goes on here on the island but at nighttime they haven't been using the heavy artillery.

Wednesday, November 18, 1942

Really a nice day today. So quiet and peaceful. Nothing happening of any importance. We can't write any mail until further notice. Things are getting too quiet around here. There's a lot of scuttlebutt about leaving here soon but I don't know. We've been hearing that for the past three months.

Thursday, November 19, 1942

Well, I received a letter today from Reta in New Zealand and I also received a package from her with a cigarette case for Christmas in it. We can write mail again now. Latest dope is we go to New Zealand in around two weeks. We are crating our stuff now and drawing clothes, etc. The cigarette case sure is nice. It also has a picture of her in it.

Friday, November 20, 1942

Nothing unusual happened. C Company is going to have their own galley. Tonight is the last time we feed them. Also I received a V-mail letter from home. No air raids of any sort. The outcome of the sea battle was 28 Jap ships sunk and our losses were two cruisers and six destroyers, which was quite a victory for us.

Saturday, November 21, 1942

Well, it really rained today; continuously all day long. Ships came in today, two big cargo ships and a couple of barges, plus four destroyers. One was the *Betelgeuse* and the *Libra*. Army is taking over the commissary and the rest of the stuff now. So I guess it won't be long before we're shoving off again. Val left, and Martin too, to cook over in C Company as they are having their own separate mess.

Sunday, November 22, 1942

Ships came back in again today. Really giving it to those Japs now. All our planes are bombing and strafing the Japs up at the other end of the island. Fortresses, dive bombers, torpedo planes and Air Cobras. Made a handle for my bayonet out of mahogany. Sure was a nice day all day long. The sunrises and sunsets are surely beautiful.

Monday, November 23, 1942

Another real nice day. No air raids at all. Long time no see Japanese airplane. Two cargo ships still here with their escorts. Foster paid me $85.00; now owes me $11.00. Collected $2.00 off Clark. Lent Olrine $1.00. Dope is, A Company is supposed to leave within two days. No dates can be named in letters and also we're not allowed to tell where we are anymore. We know that we will be leaving the island very shortly.

Tuesday, November 24, 1942

Nothing happened today of any importance. I felt pretty bad. Headache all day, weak and sick to my stomach, so I laid in my sack all day long. Looks like we're going to celebrate Thanksgiving on the island but that's alright too. So ends another uneventful day in Guadalcanal Island.

Wednesday, November 25, 1942

Well, A Company is now standing by on one hour notice. In other words, they can be told at 5:00 P.M. to be ready to leave at 6:00 P.M. and have to be ready. Nothing happened during the day much. Our artillery is really shelling the Japs up in the hills now and numerous fires can be seen up in the hills. Our boys buried two Marines and 29 soldiers that got killed up in the hills. Around 2:35 A.M. this morning, three Jap twin-motored bombers came over and killed six cooks in the 1st Marines and wounded around 18 men.

Thursday, November 26, 1942

Well, around 4:05 A.M. this morning, the Dirty Little Brown Brothers came over and dropped 15 bombs. So far I haven't received any report on the damage done. Well, today is Thanksgiving. I'm sure thankful that I'm still alive. A Company received word that they are going to draw $100.00 when we hit New Zealand. Had our pictures taken the other day of the whole outfit. Also I sent home a letter to the folks. Later on I received a V-mail from Jeanne.

Friday, November 27, 1942

At 4:00 A.M. this morning, I woke up and heard Jap planes above us. The anti-aircraft cut loose; the searchlights were on and then he cut loose with his bombs. Went back to bed; just got in my sack and he came back and dropped another load. One hit down on the beach. Johnson is taking my sword and bayonet for me. I hope he doesn't lose it or anything. I received a V-mail letter from Mother. Also we got a dozen turkeys in. A Company was supposed to go aboard ship today but they decided to let B Medical go in their place. Some of the boys feel pretty bad about it.

Saturday, November 28, 1942

Louie came over early this morning but we had some planes up so he didn't drop any eggs. For breakfast we had a fresh orange apiece. One of our cargo ships is burning out there; they say it took a torpedo in her. It was a torpedo and the ship was the *Alchiba.* Three soldiers were killed when they dove off the side and got caught in the propeller screw. Had our Thanksgiving meal today: fresh turkey, apple pie, fresh mashed potatoes, dressing, and lemonade. For breakfast we each had an orange. Ammunition exploding on the ship all day long. I was down on the beach watching the ship burn. More ships are supposed to come in tomorrow.

Sunday, November 29, 1942

Well, our buddy "One Lung Louis" came over this morning and dropped six large bombs. Also around dawn five transport ships came in. We had 11 ships out there that I could see. I guess they were trying to get that sub. At around 9:00 A.M., depth charges started going off and the ground shook underfoot! Army troops were coming off that were at Pearl Harbor. Our big guns (on land) started firing up into the hills again and I hear they're making a big drive up there now.

Monday, November 30, 1942

Well, we didn't have Louie give us reveille this morning which didn't piss me off. Had a bad wind; blowing nearly all day long and then it started raining hard. Gee, everything good happened today. I got a letter from Mother, Dad, Margaret Ann, and the Aurora Men's Club. We got fresh eggs, fresh butter, and meat. "Pork chops." Boy, fresh food and mail both in one day is almost too much. Like the fattening of the cow before the kill. We got fresh butter, eggs, oatmeal, and meat. Just like back home in the pre-war days.

Tuesday, December 1, 1942

Well, I received no mail today when it came in but probably next time I will. No more word of when we are going to leave. Had some kind of a sea battle last night. Jap cans landed 300 Japs right where the Army landed the day before. They were unprepared for combat and all 300 were wiped out. Early this morning, Louie came over and circled around for about ¾ of an hour but didn't drop anything as it was very cloudy and visibility was very poor.

Wednesday, December 2, 1942

In the sea battle, we lost one can and two cruisers damaged and got 14 Jap ships. Started pounding the Japs in the hills again, planes bombing and artillery going to town. Rained all afternoon and on and off all night long. No more dope on going home. *Alchiba,* they saved the mail and got it off today. Now have a British mine sweeper out here too.

Thursday, December 3, 1942

Well, Louie didn't come over this morning. Tojo must be slipping. Sent home three Christmas cards today. Eleven ships came in this morning; four of which were cargo and transports. Also our advanced echelon is supposed to leave tonight. Lane is leaving with them. Little made staff sergeant today. Again they tell us we will be leaving shortly. Of course we're bound to go back to the States eventually if we live long enough. Had an air raid alarm around 7:00 P.M. but it was just some of our planes coming in.

Friday, December 4, 1942

Well, today makes 119 days on the island. Had an air raid around 3:00 A.M. but no bombs were dropped. Twenty-three planes raided Bouganville. We lost one plane. Of the 14 Jap ships, five were transports, seven were destroyers and two were cruisers and possibly two more destroyers sunk. Report today that we've sunk five more Jap ships. Thirty Jap survivors were picked up floating around in the ocean. Seven died of exposure, 23 are yet alive. Japs up in the hills are really catching it now. Getting Jap patrols, etc., that have left the main body of Japs. They haven't arms, food, or supplies. They're living off the island.

Saturday, December 5, 1942

Louie didn't come over this morning; I missed him. It's getting awful dull around here now; no air raids or shellings. It's too peaceful. Maybe something will happen tomorrow; it's Sunday and that's Japs day. Oh yes, it was reported that our Navy got three subs yesterday.

Sunday, December 6, 1942

Nice weather, nothing doing of any importance. Breski and I went out in the boondocks and got us some mahogany and started making some swagger sticks. Got some good pieces of mahogany and a few good ideas. I hope they turn out alright.

Monday, December 7, 1942

It's been reported that a big sea battle is taking place about 150 miles from Guadalcanal Island. But we have received no information on the outcome. A sub put another torpedo in the *Alchiba* in the stern and it's sinking and I guess this time they won't try to repair it. They said we get mail tomorrow; I hope so.

Tuesday, December 8, 1942

Well, our advanced echelon left today so I guess we'll be leaving here pretty soon. Finished my swagger stick today. I guess we're going to leave the beach either today or tomorrow, so they say. They said the 8th Marines are going relieve us of the beach defense. Weather is real nice. I also ordered some pictures we had taken of us down at the beach here. 5th Marines leaving tomorrow, that is the remainder of them.

Wednesday, December 9, 1942

Well, the 11th Marines went aboard ship last night. The Captain said at breakfast in this area that we would move down to Red Beach and stand by for embarkation. I got my Christmas present yesterday; three cartons of cigarettes, Christmas cards, and some V-mail forms and a pen and pencil set. Boy, I'll sure be glad to leave here; it's starting to get pretty monotonous. Also we had two air raids.

Thursday, December 10, 1942

Nothing happened today exciting. I got my birthday package from home and a letter from Eileen and one from Millie Mock. The scuttlebutt is still going around about us leaving but I still think we'll be here for Christmas or maybe even later than that.

Friday, December 11, 1942

So far nothing has happened today of any interest. After dark last night, we really had a rainstorm which was the worst one we have had since being on the island. The thunder sounded just like naval gunfire and there was lightning continuously. I received three letters from Reta and one from Jeanne and Ray. Twelve Jap destroyers are headed this way and Jap planes; expecting a gas attack. Orders to check all gas masks. Planes taking out after them now. Hope they get them. We got beer; two bottles apiece.

Saturday, December 12, 1942

Well, I've been in the service for 11 months. A little better than six months overseas. Had an air raid around 8:00 A.M. this morning to start the morning off right. Paid $3.00 for beer; that's 20 bottles and the $2.00 change I lost due to a hole in my pants pocket. Today we got four apiece. Our planes got four of the destroyers and our PT boat got one.

Sunday, December 13, 1942

Around 2:00 A.M. we had an air raid. A lone Jap plane came over; they had him in the searchlights and anti-aircraft let go but they didn't get him. Two more ships in this morning. Had an air raid today at 1:00 P.M. We got mail. I received six letters. Two from the folks, one from Jeanne, two from Marge, and one from Dorthea and Lenny. Got beer; feeling good all day long. We leave here tomorrow morning. Another air raid at 10:00 P.M. Ship and land anti-aircraft let go but missed.

Monday, December 14, 1942

Well, we're supposed to leave today. All packed and ready to go. Boy, what a load I got. Second Battalion, 1st Marines are going to relieve us on the beach. We got relieved at around 10:00 A.M. and marched to the reserve area. Left there around 11:30 A.M. and went down to the beach. At approximately 1:40 P.M. we boarded the USS *Neville,* which had Doggies on. They got off and we got on. Around 2,000 Marines aboard this ship. At 8:00 P.M. we are going to Tulagi.

New Hebrides 6

Tuesday, December 15, 1942

Well, we're back at Guadalcanal again. Reported to work in the galley and boy this is really a hell hole. The heat is unbearable down there. At around 12:30 P.M. we pulled up anchor and shoved off. They say we're going to New Hebrides. Well, just one more place I haven't been. Felt good; hair tonic, shower, good soft bed pillow. Boy, what a difference; good food. What a life.

Wednesday, December 16, 1942

Well, I hear that we will be at New Hebrides tomorrow noon. I sure hope so. Boy, cold water, good food sure is good. Allies took over Burma Monday, good dope. I hope we go to New Zealand from New Hebrides and from there to the States; boy, that would be swell. Around 1:30 P.M. they started dropping depth bombs and charges to try and get a sub before he got us. I hope they got him.

Thursday, December 17, 1942

Well, today we're going to dock up at 11:00 A.M., they say. Now 10:00 A.M., approaching New Hebrides and preparing to unload the ship. Hope we don't have to go over the side on the nets. We got some real ice cream today. Boy, it sure tasted good. 1:00 P.M., the 2nd Battalion Raiders are getting off now. We don't get off until tomorrow. Saw movies and heard the Army band play for us; one number was "The Jersey Bounce." Boy, good to see and hear stuff like that.

Friday, December 18, 1942

Our advance party left ship around 7:00 A.M. Well, we left around 2:00 P.M. At 2:20 P.M. we hit the beach. Quite a bit like Guadalcanal, coconut trees and everything else. Finally got to our new camp. Set up tents in a coconut grove. On board ship, a fellow brought 100 coconuts and tried to sell them to us after all we have had and seen. Funny to be able to light cigarettes at night and see jeeps and trucks with lights on. In the evening saw Andy Hardy in *The Courtship of Andy Hardy* and then came back to camp. Saw one of our subs out in the bay. Boy, what a bunch of ships here. Saw one cruiser that had been hit; then repaired it.

Saturday, December 19, 1942

It rained nearly all night and has been raining all morning. Explored a good bit of the island. Bought a necklace of shells off one of the natives on the island. Sure is a nice place. Fresh meat every day here and fresh vegetables. In the evening saw a movie, *Dr. Christian Meets the Women,* which was a very enjoyable picture.

Sunday, December 20, 1942

Well, for one thing, we're going to draw some money. I put in for $15.00 which I think will be all I will need. Wanted to go to church but had to work. In the evening I saw two boxing matches which were pretty good and some singing imitations, etc., put on by the boys in our outfit. Also I got two bars of poggy bate.

Tuesday, December 22, 1942

Well, nothing much happened today. I saw *International Settlement* last night at the 2nd Marine area. Weather is pretty fair today. Went around the island and encountered some natives coming from the other island, in their crude boats. Bought a bracelet and some beads. Going to *Hit Parade of 1941* tonight.

Wednesday, December 23, 1942

Rained nearly all day long. Cut up a lot of meat. Eight lambs and two forequarters of beef and cleaned 22 turkeys. Got in a card game and won $6.00. In the evening we went to the show and saw *Gay Sisters;* it was a pretty good show at that.

Thursday, December 24, 1942

Well, we had turkey today for dinner, mashed potatoes, gravy, stuffing, beans, cocoa, and fruit salad; damn good meal. In the evening we had a show put on by the boys. A Navy band off the cruiser *Columbia* and nearly all the rest of the entertainment and singers were from the Amphibian Tanks.

Friday, December 25, 1942

Well, today is Christmas and on foreign soil. I went to church services this morning at 9:00 A.M. Also received orders that H & S and my Company B are going aboard ship tomorrow morning. I think we are going to Australia. Lost $10.00 playing cards today. Tell me more. Saw Andy Hardy in *The Courtship of Andy Hardy.*

Saturday, December 26, 1942

Got a native comb yesterday and a bracelet and a wild boar's tusk. Well, they say today is the day that we're to leave. That is, ½ the battalion, H & S, and good old B Company were to leave before dinner. Dinner time—still here. Late afternoon; we're to leave in the morning after breakfast. Saw Lloyd Nolan in *Blue, White and Perfect.*

Sunday, December 27, 1942

Well, we're to leave very shortly now. Around 9:00 A.M. we left camp. At approximately 10:00 A.M. we got in the Higgins boat and at 10:45 A.M. we boarded the *American Legion*. We do not have to work in the galley for the first time. Saw the Andrew Sisters in *Private Buckaroo;* had ice cream and Coca-Cola. In the evening we saw *Honky Tonk* with Clark Gable and Lana Turner.

Monday, December 28, 1942

Still in the harbor. Had a bar of candy today and ice cream and an orangeade. No movies this noon. Talk is we're leaving at 4:00 P.M. for Brisbane, Australia. Well, at exactly 4:00 P.M., we pulled up anchor and got under way. Captain told us we wouldn't be aboard the ship more than a week and we will get liberty there. *NO MOVIES.*

Tuesday, December 29, 1942

Well, we're out to sea today. At 9:00 A.M. we saw a movie, *Biscuit Eater.* At 2:00 P.M. we are having a rifle inspection. Also at 2:00 P.M. there is going to be a movie. Saw Butler, a fellow I went through boot camp with.

Wednesday, December 30, 1942

Played poker and lost. Went to the show this morning and saw *You Belong to Me,* with Barbara Stanwyck and Henry Fonda. In the afternoon I saw *Tropical Holiday,* with Dorothy Lamour and Ray Milland. Meat is terrible and clothes are wringing wet all the time. Food is bad. Washing facilities are bad; water is on 15 minutes out of the hour. Quarters are best we have on any ship. Movie line, chow line, etc. are terrible. You have to be rugged to survive.

Thursday, December 31, 1942

Well, nothing out of the ordinary. So far the voyage has been uneventful in the way of action. I saw *Hotel for Women*, with Linda Darnell. We're supposed to be in port tomorrow and get off the day after. Well, tonight will be the quietest New Year's Eve I have spent in many a year. But this is war (how well I know). Saw Mitzi Green in a Perry Mason mystery.

Books by Erle Stanley Gardner Pocket Books

No. 93, *Case of the Velvet Claws*

No. 90, *Case of the Sulky Girl*

No. 106, *Case of the Lucky Legs*

No. 116, *Case of the Howling Dog*

No. 138, *Case of the Caretaker's Cat*

No. 177, *Case of the Curious Bride*

No. 201, *Stuttering Bishop*

No. 157, *Counterfeit Eye*

Chapter 2

Liberty in Australia 7

Friday, January 1, 1943

Early this morning, land could be seen in the distance. Now 10:15 A.M. and we are quite close to the beach. Beach looks rocky and houses can be made out. Orders are to stand by to leave the ship at 3:00 P.M. Collins is in sick bay. At approximately 3:00 P.M., we docked up at Brisbane. We took nearly three hours coming up the river to the dock. Looks like beautiful country.

Saturday, January 2, 1943

Early in the morning we got under way and docked up at another dock. Liberty goes at 1:00 P.M. No dress shoes. Had a good supper, milk, lots of ice cream. Saw a show and then went dancing and did I get sick, oh boy!

Sunday, January 3, 1943

Got under way early this morning. We're going to Melbourne. Sick all day long. Couldn't keep a thing down. Wasn't from drinking, either. Got two letters from Mother and Jeanne and one from Joan, Mrs. Panger, and Audrey.

Monday, January 4, 1943

Still sick. Haven't been able to keep anything down as yet. Really is rough out today and raining. We're told we could write home and say we left Guadalcanal and on our way to a large port. Later: Really is a bad storm and the ship is tossing terrible. An awful lot of the fellows are getting sea sick.

Tuesday, January 5, 1943

Early morning weather is still very rough. Latter calmed down quite a bit. During the night it was awfully cold. Played cards and won very little, but didn't loose. Feeling a little better now. Signed up for $25.00 to be paid soon. Wrote a letter home to the folks.

Wednesday, January 6, 1943

8:20 A.M. Land is sighted. Supposed to dock at 10:00 A.M. Pack bed rolls to be ready at 9:00 A.M. Wrote to Marguerite and Mother and Jeanne. Also, one to Grace Bladeki. 1:00 P.M. and haven't docked yet. Looks like nice country; not too hilly, spotted with farms, etc. The city looks like quite the thing with high buildings, etc. 1:45 P.M. docked up. Left ship at 2:30 P.M. Greeted by a brass band. Bunked at the cricket grounds center of town. Issued six blankets and cot. Had cookies, ice cream, and candy.

Thursday, January 7, 1943

Well, we worked until 3:30 P.M. then we were told we were going to get issued clothes. Dress shoes, two pair pants, two shirts, two ties, two overseas hats, two sets of underwear, and belt and socks. Going on liberty now which expires tomorrow morning at 6:00 A.M. Dressed up we look like a bunch of Doggies with their clothes on. Only difference is the hat emblem.

Friday, January 8, 1943

Well, we just got back at 6:00 A.M.; nearly didn't make it. Orders are we are going to move. So we're going to eat chow early. Around 12:30 P.M. we left on trucks. Then boarded a train and rode for 1 ½ hours and then trucked out so far it would take a week to get back. Hear we're going to move again in the very near future. But I hope not.

Saturday, January 9, 1942

I go to work tomorrow at noon. Took off on liberty (AWOL) to Melbourne. Collins, Mac, and me. Had a swell time; plenty of women and plenty to drink. Went to a party and sure had a wonderful time.

Sunday, January 10, 1943

Came back to camp. Top Sergeant turned us in. Have to go see the man. No liberty tonight. We're now P.A.L. (prisoners at large) until we see the man. Got drunk at the slop chute. The Aussies don't make near what we do. Their ration is around .08 per day per man for food.

Monday, January 11, 1943

Today we go up for office hours at 4:00 P.M. Oh yes, we got mail today. One from Eileen and one from Marguerite. Got drunk over at the slop chute. Didn't have office hours today; postponed now until tomorrow morning. Met two swell Aussie soldiers. Bill and Bill from the last World War. They sure are two regular fellows.

Tuesday, January 12, 1943

Went to Frankston for liberty and had a pretty good time though. Up for office hours today and Collins and I were exonerated and set scott free. Met a very nice girl by the name of Ivy. She works in Melbourne at the Elizabeth Collins Café. Quite a small town, though, for the number of Marines here. Well, I've got just one year in the Marine Corps now and three more to go.

Wednesday, January 13, 1943

Went to Frankston again today for liberty; had a date with Ivy. Had a pretty good time. Nearly froze to death, though, and on top of that we went swimming. Boy, was that water cold. Those Australian women are too damn rugged for me. I guess I just can't take it.

Thursday, January 14, 1943

Walter Ikey and Little Donahey came in from New Caledonia as they have been there ever since around the 12th of August as they didn't get off the ship when we landed on the island. Going to go to Melbourne as I have liberty until 8:00 A.M. tomorrow morning. Weather is cold and raining.

Friday, January 15, 1943

Received a letter from Margaret Ann, also got paid yesterday; $50.00. Went to Frankston and bought some pictures. Had a date with Ivy. Also bought some handkerchiefs. Had a pretty good time. Money is sure going fast.

Saturday, January 16, 1943

Got my sea bag today. Also got my laundry back. Mail came in today; didn't get any as yet. Started in the NCO mess. Isn't bad cooking for around 40 men. Went to Frankston and out with Ivy. Had a pretty good time.

Sunday, January 17, 1943

Got a letter from Jeanne dated October 18th. Worked all day long in the afternoon. Lill and Ivy and Hank came out to the camp and had supper. Saw her back to the train. Going into Melbourne tomorrow at noon.

Monday, January 18, 1943

Worked until noon and then went into Melbourne with Hank and Bill Doyle and Ray. Had a date at 5:00 P.M. but didn't see her so I went out. Went to the Oxford Café and got a few quarts of wine. Also I picked up a room for the night. Had a pretty darn good time. Also I got some mail from the folks, Margaret Ann, Uncle John, Jeanne, and Marguerite and one from Eileen.

Tuesday, January 19, 1943

Met Bill, Ray, and Hank around noon at the Barclay Hotel; had a few drinks, picked up my clothes and went to meet Ivy. Had a few more drinks and went to Luna Park and then we went out on the beach for a while and then home. We all went and stayed at Vi's house.

Wednesday, January 20, 1943

Woke up and Vi had breakfast for us. We then took the girls to work and I caught a train back to camp. Got paid 30 pounds. Also got mail. Received stationary from Auntie and Uncle Jack. Letters from Marguerite; two. Myron two and one from the folks and one from Margaret Ann in the afternoon. I had a quart of Black and White Scotch given to me plus plenty of beer. That's all. (That's enough).

Thursday, January 21, 1943

Worked from 5:00 A.M. till 6:30 P.M., then I started drinking and playing cards until around 11:30 P.M. Then it was time to go to bed. Wrote several letters (17) but they won't be mailed as the censor stamp has been lost.

Friday, January 22, 1943

Worked until noon and took off for Melbourne and got a room with Mrs. Walters, a very nice woman. In the evening I left Charlie and went into town and met a very sweet girl by the name of Dorothy and had a wonderful time. Going home, I sprained my ankle but didn't care as it was *worth it*.

Saturday, January 23, 1943

Had breakfast at Mrs. Walters' and then went to town. Had a shave and haircut and a *few beers*. Then Charlie and I went to the Bentleigh and over to Dot's. Went to Melbourne and to a dance at the Trocadero and another lovely evening was spent.

Sunday, January 24, 1943

Stayed at Dot's all night (slept alone) then went to Melbourne. Got my things and address where my watch was. Came back to Bentleigh. Should have been back to camp at 1:00 P.M. but wasn't. But I think it was worth the consequences. Back to camp 13 hours late.

Monday, January 25, 1943

Back to the old grind today. Marines are having a parade the 22nd of February. Bought U.S. cigarettes, first time since we've been here. Received a letter and Christmas card from Reta. Long time no letter. Hope I can get liberty by Thursday as I sure have a lot of things to do. Plus my watch, which I have to get back. Had quite a bit of beer (more than enough), oh boy! What a life.

Tuesday, January 26, 1943

Found out that my greens arrived but somebody beat me to them. May close the NCO mess over the weekend. I sure hope so. Had a few beers again today. I also got two sets of khakis. Mailed 13 letters; I hope they go out soon. Also 35 replacements arrived today and more are supposed to come in. McDonald went to the hospital as he got a dose. Second one as he got it in New Caledonia.

Wednesday, January 27, 1943

Worked until noon and then I went into Melbourne and met Dot. We went to the show and saw *To the Shores of Tripoli,* and it was a very good show. Then went to Dot's and stayed there till—

Thursday, January 28, 1943

Had breakfast at Dot's and then went into town with her. Supposed to be back at camp at noon but I didn't make it. So in the evening I went back to Dot's and she was kind of peeved but she got over it.

Friday, January 29, 1943

Still didn't get my watch back but I hope I do, or at least I better. Still did not get back to camp. But I will one of these days. Going back to camp tomorrow. Went out with Dot and saw *Joan of Paris*, and then went home to Dot's.

Saturday, January 30, 1943

Going back to camp today. Went into Melbourne with Dot this morning. Met Roy and I didn't get back to camp, so we had a party. Boy, what a time we had.

Sunday, January 31, 1943

Started back to camp but I didn't quite make it. Went to Parkdale with Roy and Joe. Then we went back to Melbourne on the last train. Boy, have I got a cold and do I feel lousy. Oh! Boy!

Monday, February 1, 1943

Came back to camp at last. Left Melbourne on the 6:30 A.M. train. Got back to camp and Teddy was sick so I didn't even have time to change clothes but started right into work. He had malaria so they took him to the hospital. Davis went over the weekend. Collins and Eurlick are going tomorrow along with Burnel, he got yellow jaundice. Got those pictures we took on Esperanto Santos from Collins today; they only cost three shillings. So ends another day.

Tuesday, February 2, 1943

So we are on the second month of '43. But I don't feel any too good. Didn't get my watch yet; he can't find it. Worked the same as usual; got a few letters today. Walter and I went into Parksdale. I had a date with Bertha. Had a pretty fair time. Nearly missed the train back.

Wednesday, February 3, 1943

Worked until noon today. They took Miller away from me and gave me Smitty from A. MCD. Went into Melbourne with Frank but didn't have a date or get one as I just didn't want one for a change. Had champagne for the first time in my life. Also got my watch back. £1 is the cost. New back and crystal and cleaned. Also a new tailor-made hat for 11 and 6.

Thursday, February 4, 1943

Went into Melbourne with Bill Meyer and I met a nice girl; have a date with her tomorrow; name Janette. We went out with Jeanne and Beryll Opri and we really had a very good time. Boy, what women they have out here. Had some more champagne and sauterne wine plus one quart of whiskey, then to Luna Park—. Everybody was conscious. Women do just about everything over here. And prices are a little bit higher over here.

Friday, February 5, 1943

Well, got back to camp at around 6:45 A.M. Boy, I really feel all worn out; much more of this and I don't know. Four letters from the folks and four from Reta in New Zealand. Got my laundry back and bought some new shoes in Melbourne yesterday for 30 not quite £2 anyhow. Went to Melbourne, had a date with Janette; went out to Luna Park. Got to get some sleep pretty soon. Saw Val Tyson while I was waiting for my date and didn't remember her.

Saturday, February 6, 1943

Worked all day long; had a date in Morellica but went to Bentleigh instead and saw Dot. She wasn't home so I waited. She came home with a Platoon Sergeant from the 5th Marines. Boy, do I need sleep.

Sunday, February 7, 1943

Well, I got off at noon today and went to see Dot. Five minutes after I got there, that Platoon Sergeant called but upon finding me there, he left. So I stayed all day and spent the night there.

Monday, February 8, 1943

Went into Melbourne with Dot in the morning but didn't go back to camp. Saw the picture show, *Wake Island*, which was very good. Got my pants pressed and mended. Went over to see Val Tyson. Bought a couple of pins for souvenirs. Had a date with Beryll in the evening. Jean & Bill and Beryll and myself went out and had a pretty good time.

Tuesday, February 9, 1943

No sleep. Waited from 1:00 A.M. until 5:00 A.M. for a train back to camp and back to the old grind. Went to bed around 8:00 A.M. and slept until 11:30 A.M. Pete came back from the hospital and Eurlick went. Wrote a few letters back home. Then went to bed around 10:30 P.M. I got some sleep for a change. Wrote a letter to Beryll and Bill wrote one to Jean.

Wednesday, February 10, 1943

Still hard at work. I get off tomorrow at noon. Also got paid today. Received $64.50. In other words, I received £20. Boy, at this rate I'll be paid and not have a cent left. Val took over charge of the mess this morning. They relieved Little. Too bad, he's a good man too. Called up Beryll today and I am going to call her again tonight. Also got two more mess men. Presky is coming over here tomorrow as my relief. Walter paid the £3 he owed me too.

Thursday, February 11, 1943

Well I worked until noon today and then I went on liberty to Melbourne. I received a permanent liberty card. Met Dot at work. Ski was with me. She got her girlfriend Vi for him. Boy, what a beauty she is. Oh boy! Had a pretty good time. Stayed at Dot's all night.

Friday, February 12, 1943

Went into town with Dot. Left her at work and met Bill at 11:15 A.M. Bought one quart of whiskey and three small bottles of brandy. Had my picture taken and cabled home $60.00. Went to dinner and then out to Luna Park. Then did I get sick, oh boy! So Beryll made me catch a train back to camp. So I spoiled a whole evening, darn it!

Saturday, February 13, 1943

Well I got back to camp around 2:30 A.M. this morning. Slept until noon; still don't feel any too well. Paid Collins £1. Sure is a nice day today. Wish it was March, then she will be down here. Boy, she sure is a swell girl. What a life.

Sunday, February 14, 1943

Well, I worked all day today. Boy, I sure hated to work on a beautiful day like this. Oh well, I'm going on liberty tomorrow. Received £1. 5 and 0 for the last two weeks work here. Every little bit helps, more or less.

Monday, February 15, 1943

Worked until noon today and then went to Melbourne. Had a date with Beryll, but she told me she couldn't go out and why. Oh well, such is life. Met another girl and had a pretty good time. Got a room in the hotel and stayed there all night. So ends another day in Melbourne.

Tuesday, February 16, 1943

Met Bill and saw a show with Ray Milland and Claudette Colbert. In the afternoon, I met Ted, Frank, and Davis and we started drinking champagne; we killed eight bottles at £1 per bottle. Then Frank and I got dates and we went out to Luna Park. I had a pretty good time. The girl was very nice, name of Mary. Meeting her Friday night. Slept in the train overnight as I missed the last one back to camp.

Wednesday, February 17, 1943

Arrived in camp around 6:45 A.M., ate breakfast and then went to bed till around 11:00 A.M. Came to work and it's sure tough to have to stay in. They took Donahey to the hospital yesterday. Received several letters today; three from Eileen, around four from the folks and one from Jeanne and one from Joan. Going to a little party tonight some of the boys are having in camp.

Thursday, February 18, 1943

Well, I had to work all day today. Last night I called up Beryll and talked to her for about 15 minutes. Boy, she sure is a swell girl. Also received two letters from home today and a *Cleveland Press* with my picture in it in blues. Then I got my laundry and finished work and wrote some letters home. Hoff and Davis came out to see me for a little while today. Price got sick today.

Friday, February 19, 1943

Worked until noon today and then I went into Melbourne and met Mary. But I got half looped first and saw Val first; she is a nice kid. In the evening, Mary and I saw *Remember Pearl Harbor,* which was a fair show. Went out to some town hall and stayed all night.

Saturday, February 20, 1943

Met Val at 1:00 P.M. and I got pretty tight before I met her. Went out to the house and met her mother. Went to Luna Park in the evening. Went out to the town hall again in the evening.

Sunday, February 21, 1943

Came back to Melbourne and then went to Frankston. Val wasn't there. Met Christine. She had to go back. Then I met Joy and I really had a good time. Got back to camp around 9:30 P.M.

Monday, February 22, 1943

Well, it's George Washington's birthday today. The boys are parading in Melbourne today and here I am working. Got letters from Mrs. Panger, Mrs. Peterson, Marguerite, Reta, and also a Christmas package from Eileen and one from Mother. Cigarettes, candy, gum, newspapers, and fruit cake. In the evening I wrote letters and I also called up Beryll.

Tuesday, February 23, 1943

Well, I worked until noon today and then went into town. I went and saw Val. Then I left her as I had a date. Missed my date as I arrived too late. Bumped into Dot and took her out. Had a little disagreement so I came back to camp. I had to anyway as we get paid tomorrow.

Wednesday, February 24, 1943

Got paid £20 today. Val and I went into Melbourne together. He's got a room out at St. Kilda. I went out with Joy. Had a pretty good time. We went to the show and saw *Joan of Paris.*

Thursday, February 25, 1943

Stayed at the American Red Cross all night. I called Val and then I went out there. We hung around town and had quite a few drinks. Then in the evening, Beryll and I and Jean and Bill went out to celebrate Bill and Jean's birthday. Drank four quarts of champagne and had a really good time.

Friday, February 26, 1943

Bill and I stayed at the Red Cross again last night. Met Ski. He and I went out to see Val. Then the three of us took off for Melbourne. I bought an officer's khaki cap for 12/s. In the evening, I had a date with Chris; we went to a show then I went back out and stayed with Val all night.

Saturday, February 27, 1943

Went in town with Val and Ski. Then I went to see Beryll but she had a date so then I bumped into Florence and went out with her and to her place. Then went to sleep and went out with Betty at 2:30 A.M. till 6:15 A.M.

Sunday, February 28, 1943

Saw Betty at 10:00 A.M. till around 12:30 P.M. At 2:00 P.M. Val and I left as I had a date at 2:30 P.M. with Joy. Went for a ride on the river. At 10:15 she got a train to work; at 10:20 I got a train back to camp.

Monday, March 1, 1943

Well, back to the old grind again. Got a letter from home. Lane came back today. Galloway made Marine gunner. Training period is going to start. Liberty now goes from 5:00 P.M. until 12:00 P.M. but that doesn't include cooks, thank God! Saw Tebbe yesterday and had my picture taken with Joy.

Tuesday, March 2, 1943

Worked until noon today. Then I went into town. Met a girl by the name of Joyce and then I met Reta. Later on I went out with Florence. At 12:00 P.M. I went out and saw Betty. Boy, these women sure keep a fellow busy. Stayed there till about 6:30 A.M.

Wednesday, March 3, 1943

Left Betty's at 6:30 A.M., then I went to the city. I met Ski when I went to breakfast. We went out to Betty's in the afternoon. Ski went to see Ivy but she was busy. Betty is really starting to get it bad. What women they have in this country. I bought an emu egg today for 10/s 6/0. It sure is nice.

Thursday, March 4, 1943

Well, I left at around 7:30 A.M. but I had to see Betty before I left. Got back at noon and went to work. Got letters from Mrs. Peterson, Marguerite, and the folks. In the evening, Frank Berger and myself went to the dance in Frankston. We really had a swell time too. What a crazy bunch we are. Poor girls. Drawing £85, which is $247.82 in good old U.S. money.

Friday, March 5, 1943

Well, I have to work all day today. But I am going into Frankston tonight and meet Beryll, Bill, and Jeanne at 7:00 P.M. Went over to Mount Martha and we all had a party. Started on sauterne wine, then beer, then whiskey, brandy, and ended up on port wine and that just about ended me up too.

Saturday, March 6, 1943

Boy, I sure am tired. Got in at 3:15 A.M.; started work at 5:00 A.M. I have a date with Beryll at 1:00 P.M. We went to Mornington and then came back to Mount Martha. We had some to drink and spent the evening there.

Sunday, March 7, 1943

Date with Beryll again. We had six quarts of beer but it sure didn't last long. We were down on the beach all afternoon. Jeanne and Bill went back to Melbourne. We ate dinner down there again, on the girls. They sure are some girls.

Monday, March 8, 1943

Worked from noon until evening. Then I went down to see Beryll again. There is a girl I would like to marry. I really mean it. We had three quarts of beer which she paid for plus one bottle of burgundy. We talked nearly all evening. I stayed there till around 2:00 A.M. I got back to camp at 3:15 A.M. and had to go to work at 4:30 A.M.

Tuesday, March 9, 1943

Boy, I sure am tired today; only an hour's sleep all night and besides I've got a date with Beryll again tonight. Nearly all day long you could hear the cruisers target practicing out in the ocean. Just like on the island, only this time we did not have to worry. Received mail from Jeanne, Mrs. Peterson, folks, Marguerite, and two letters from Reta.

Wednesday, March 10, 1943

Well, I worked until noon today and then Berger and I took off for Melbourne. We went to The Australia for drinks and then had supper and met the girls. Went to the Embassy and danced till around 1:30 A.M. and then took the girls home. Had a pretty good time.

Thursday, March 11, 1943

Well, first off I had to see the doctor about my throat. Then I had to go and get paid. I drew £85 ($274.38), which isn't hay. Went down to see Beryll in the afternoon. We went to the dance in Frankston in the evening and then I took her home but of course I stayed there for a short time. Received a letter from Mother and one from Dad.

Friday, March 12, 1943

Well the camp is pretty well deserted today as everybody is on leave. Started at noon and will work until Monday. In the evening, we played cards and I lost about 2 1/2 £. So it really didn't pay to stay in camp.

Saturday, March 13, 1943

Worked all day today. In the evening Berger and I went into Melbourne to a party but it was called off so I came back to camp. Met an Aussie warrant officer, Tom White.

Sunday, March 14, 1943

Worked until noon and then I went to East Oakleigh to see Tom White and had a fairly nice time. Talked, had supper and a few drinks.

Monday, March 15, 1943

Well, I slept until noon today and then I went into Melbourne. I called up Beryll and Lois, and Joy. Tess and I saw Reta and Val Tyson but I made a date with Doris but she had to go away as her mother got sick. And Betty is on her vacation so that's that.

Tuesday, March 16, 1943

Back to camp and back to work. Nothing happened but then you couldn't expect too much being in camp.

Wednesday, March 17, 1943

Well, I worked all day long today. In the evening I went into Melbourne as I had a date with Lill, my little (A.W.A.S.) girl. We went to the rodeo and had a fairly nice time. Boy, was I tired.

Thursday, March 18, 1943

Worked until noon today and then Val and I went into Melbourne. I called up Betty and made a date with her. In the evening saw Betty for the last time. So ends Betty, but she was getting too serious.

Friday, March 19, 1943

Met Val and Bill this morning, then I met a girl by the name of Amy and we went out till around 4:00 P.M. Then I met Susanne and was with her till

7:30 P.M. At 8:15, I met Lois and was with her till 11:45 P.M. What a day I put in.

Saturday, March 20, 1943

Back in camp at 7:00 A.M. this morning. I think I'm going out tonight after work if she's home. Berger and I went into the Trocadero in the evening. I met an A.W.A.S. girl by the name of Margaret. Have a date with her for Tuesday.

Sunday, March 21, 1943

Worked until noon today, then Berger and I went into Melbourne. I had a date with Amy. He got Frances and we went out together and had a swell time.

Monday, March 22, 1943

Well, I worked until noon today and then Bob and I went into Melbourne and I dated Betty Fisher. Went to the dance. Bob didn't have a date but went to the dance with us. Received a couple of letters today from home and one from Irene.

Tuesday, March 23, 1943

Well, I had a date with Betty at 1:45 P.M. and went to the show. Saw *Man in the Truck* and *Tuxedo Junction*. Was with her until 7:00 P.M. then I went out with Margaret. Went out to Luna Park and then took her back to camp.

Wednesday, March 24, 1943

Well, I'm back in camp again but not for long as I have a date with Lois to go to the picture show. Received more mail from home and another from Irene.

Thursday, March 25, 1943

Well, I'm not doing nothing this weeknight as I am staying in camp tonight. As I haven't had any sleep and also financial difficulties.

Friday, March 26, 1943

Well, I worked until noon today and then I took off for Melbourne; had a date with Amy but she wasn't there and I met Lorna and took her out and I sure had a swell time.

Saturday, March 27, 1943

Well, I went out with Lorna in the afternoon and then I went into Melbourne, didn't see Bob; things were called off. Went out to Luna Park and met Joan, then went back to Luna and met Lorna and took her home.

Sunday, March 28, 1943

Well, I slept until about 11:00 A.M. then I went out and saw Amy. I was with her and we went to the museum and had supper and then to the park and then to her house and back to camp.

Monday, March 29, 1943

Back to the old grind once more. Seems kinda funny to work all day long. Sent home Japanese ½ shilling, one shell, 10 yen, and 50 yen. Sent one shilling to Irene. Tomorrow we draw clothes, also H, S, and L Companies. A Company left today to go on maneuvers. In the evening, Bob and I went into the dance at Frankston. Made an appointment with the dentist for 10:00 A.M. tomorrow morning.

Tuesday, March 30, 1943

Well, I finally got my tooth filled by the dentist and he sure did a swell job. Drew new pair of green pants, two flannel shirts, and two sets of heavy underwear. Mailed home some letters. Then I went into Melbourne and went to see Amy and we went out. I used Val's cottage and stayed there all night.

Wednesday, March 31, 1943

Well, Val woke me up and then we went to get a haircut. Got picked up by the MPs for being out of uniform and also for wearing sergeant chevrons. Then in the evening, I had a date with Betty. I saw *Glass Key* and *My Favorite Blonde*. Then Betty and I went to the Trocadero and had a fair time. Met Bill and we slept at the Red Cross.

Thursday, April 1, 1943

Well, I came back to camp this morning and signed the payroll for $80.70. Also I sent home Jap money. £1, 1/2s, newspapers clipping, Jap postcard, nine photos taken on the island, and one photo of Reta in New Zealand and a Jap beer label. In the afternoon, I called up Beryll.

Friday, April 2, 1943

Called up Beryll today and am going out tonight. But I will have to get the last train back to camp. We went to the movies and had tea and then I took her home and came back to camp.

Saturday, April 3, 1943

Well, I got paid today £25. Also Paul Breski paid me back £2 and Bob and I went in and I got happy. Met Veronica. Lost all my clothes and ended up at the Gladstone House.

Sunday, April 4, 1943

Bob and I went back to camp. I got a green blouse for 10/s and we went into Melbourne. I had a date with Betty and he with Frances. Went out for supper and then we went to the Coconut Grove and danced and I had a very good time.

Monday, April 5, 1943

Well, I came back to camp. Got to the dentist too late and missed my appointment. Got a shot for typhoid fever. Bob didn't come back; they put him on report at noon. I went into Frankston but got back to camp around 9:30 P.M. and went to bed.

Tuesday, April 6, 1943

Worked all day. Bob still didn't come back to camp. They had a dance in camp for the Amphibian Tractor Battalion, so I went over with the boys and had a fair time.

Wednesday, April 7, 1943

Well, I worked until noon today and then I went into town with Frank F. Went out and saw Frances and then I went to see Lorna but she was sick so I went to see Amy and we went to the pictures. We saw *Mrs. Miniver,* and then came home. Received a letter from Mrs. Peterson and what it contained was somewhat of a shock.

Thursday, April 8, 1943

Well, Frank and I had a few drinks and stayed around town till afternoon and then went to the pictures and saw *Submarine Raiders,* and we also saw

South American George. Took Betty home and went back to the hotel. Received a letter from Beryll.

Friday, April 9, 1943

Well, back in camp and to work again. We didn't close the galley down as we have to stay open for now; and it was our turn to close the galley down too. Have a date in Frankston tonight by the name of Mary. Went to the show and then I came back to camp. Got home around 12:30 A.M.

Saturday, April 10, 1943

My dentist wasn't there yesterday, but I have an appointment with him for 1:30 P.M. on Monday. Stayed in camp and spent a very dull evening.

Sunday, April 11, 1943

Well, I worked until noon today and then I went into Melbourne. Didn't have a date. I went in and saw Frances and spent the evening there slinging the bull.

Monday, April 12, 1943

Well, I worked and then I took off for Melbourne. I had a date with Lorna so I met her around 5:30 P.M. and then we went out for supper and the evening. I had a very nice time. It sure was cold, though.

Tuesday, April 13, 1943

Didn't wake up until nearly 1:00 P.M., then I went in town, had dinner and went to the pictures. I saw Abbot and Costello in *Ride 'Em Cowboy,* then went to meet Betty. We went to the show and saw *Syncopation* and *Thundering West.*

Wednesday, April 14, 1943

Well, I came back to camp this morning. I received some mail. I got three letters and one V-mail from Irene P. and one from Margaret and one from Irene Yambor. Went to the show with Bob but as I had already seen it, I didn't stay. Put the evening in talking with the boys and go to bed early.

Thursday, April 15, 1943

Well, I went into town today. I waited till around 2:00 P.M. but it didn't stop raining so I went in anyhow. Met a very nice redhead by the name of Val

Benson. In the evening, I went out with Betty and had a very nice time, only I got soaked and nearly froze to death.

Friday, April 16, 1943

Came back to camp to sign the payroll and then went back to the city. I received a letter from Irene, three from the folks, and two from Eileen. Saw Betty but she was busy so I went to Luna Park on my own. I met a WAF by the name of Carman. Had a pretty good time.

Saturday, April 17, 1943

Well, I came back to camp today at noon. My warrant has been sent in to get changed. Wrote letters in the evening as I had nothing else to do. Cold and raining, sure miserable.

Sunday, April 18, 1943

Worked until noon and then I went into Melbourne. Betty wasn't there so I went to Prahran and saw Amy. She is going away for good to become a nurse; so ends Amy.

Monday, April 19, 1943

Went into Melbourne at noon or I should say late afternoon as I had an appointment with the dentist at 1:30 P.M. Paid at 11:15 A.M. Then had time to see the movie, *Next of Kin,* in camp. Had a date with Norma. Really had a swell time.

Tuesday, April 20, 1943

Came back to camp to see the dentist. I have to see him again Friday for the last time. Went back to Melbourne and went to the show. Saw *Ball of Fire,* which was very good. Then I met Betty at 11:00 P.M. and met her mother. Went out to eat and then home. Had a good time; she is a swell kid. Drew an M-1, a sweater and two pair of socks.

Wednesday, April 21, 1943

Rented the cottage Val used to have and then I came back to camp. Val got himself in a nice jam. Received a letter from Jeanne and Ray today. Frank is going in with me on the cottage. McDonald got busted and has a Summary Court Martial coming. Bob Berger is getting a Deck Court Martial. Cleaned my new rifle in the evening and went to bed around 9:00 P.M.

Thursday, April 22, 1943

Raining again today. It seems like that's all it's done in the last two weeks, is rain. Also it's pretty damn cold, in fact, I'm about frozen. Got some mail; one from Jeanne and Ray, Eileen, and three from the folks. Got feeling happy during the evening.

Friday, April 23, 1943

Well, I worked until noon today and then I took off on liberty to Melbourne. Ike started to work here. Met Betty but she was sick, so I took off. Went to the dance down at Palm Grove and had a fairly good time.

Saturday, April 24, 1943

Well Frank and I went to a hotel he knows and started drinking. We met two conductors that work on the trams. I stayed with the one all afternoon and evening. Frank left as he had a date.

Sunday, April 25, 1943

Well I saw the parade in town and God what a crowd there was. Couldn't make any connections so I called up Tess and went out to her place. En route to Melbourne, I met a nice girl, name of Helen, and going back to camp, another one, Lorna.

Monday, April 26, 1943

Well, I'm back to the old grind again. But I have to go into Melbourne tonight and from there to Moonee Ponds. I had two letters from the folks. One from Irene, one from Margaret Ann, and one from Joan. It sure is good to receive mail. Boy, what a life. Went to Melbourne and out with Helen and had a pretty good time.

Tuesday, April 27, 1943

Well, I worked until noon today and then I went into Melbourne with Palermo. Got hit by a truck; nothing serious, luckily, just got side swiped and knocked about 20 yards. My back sure was bothered though. Went and saw Ruby; didn't go out, just stayed at her place all evening.

Wednesday, April 28, 1943

Well, I got my shoes soled and heeled finally. I went and saw Lorna in the afternoon and evening until around 9:00 A.M. when I received word I was to report back to camp as soon as possible. Around 10:00 P.M. I called up Fran and went up there to see her and I didn't get back to camp.

Thursday, April 29, 1943

Well, I just missed a lot of trains today, but I did manage to catch the one at 11:13 P.M. and got back into camp around 1:30 A.M. But everybody was asleep. Breski went to the hospital with blood poisoning.

Friday, April 30, 1943

Well, Bernie is taking Breski's place. I'm going out to the rifle range and fire an M-1 today. Left around 10:00 A.M. and got out there around noon. Ate dinner and then fired preliminaries and then for record. I didn't do any too good. I made 154 out of a possible 200. Came back to camp and then went on liberty to Melbourne. Called up Fran and took her out.

Saturday, May 1, 1943

Came back to camp around 10:00 A.M. Going to see the doctor about my back today, it sure bothers me a hell of a lot. The folks received four Jap bills I sent home to them. Wrote seven letters which was a night's work.

Sunday, May 2, 1943

My back is still bothering me quite a bit. Don't know if I will go on liberty at noon or not. Went to Melbourne and went out with Ruby, sure had a swell time.

Monday, May 3, 1943

Worked until noon today and went into Melbourne. Got my watch fixed and also got my ring back. Went up to see Fran and had a pretty good time. Played poker and then went out and had steak around 10:30 P.M.

Tuesday, May 4, 1943

Frank woke me up and we went into town and met the boys. Collins, Davis, Tebbe, Maraldo, Goldman, Palermo, and Frueher, and boy, did they get me drunk. Then I went to see Betty and she was busy so I went to see Dot H. and I took her out. A good time was had by all.

Wednesday, May 5, 1943

Well, I came back to camp today and I sure didn't feel any too good. Also, I got the picture that our company took on the island and then I got paid £10. Supposed to go out tonight but I sure don't feel like it so I'm going to stay in camp.

Thursday, May 6, 1943

Well, I went into Melbourne and met Frank at Ruby's house. He and one Ruby went out, the other one and I stayed home. Got peeved, told her to go to ____ and shoved off and went to Fran and had a pretty good time, only I had to get the last train.

Friday, May 7, 1943

Well, I took off at noon and went into Melbourne, had a date with Betty at 4:00 P.M. and went and had a few drinks and then ate and went to the show. Saw *A Yank at Eton.* Had a nice time.

Saturday, May 8, 1943

Met a nice girl by the name of Valeria. Twenty-three, blonde, beautiful build. Left her at 4:30, went and had supper, and then went out to see Fran and we stayed home but had a nice time.

Sunday, May 9, 1943

Was with her all day. Around 6:00 P.M. we went out and had supper and went to the cottage till around 11:00 P.M. as I had to get back to camp.

Monday, May 10, 1943

Well, back in the old swing of things again. Not that I want to be. Had a letter from Mike, the folks, and Eileen and Uncle John. Raining all day, very miserable weather.

Tuesday, May 11, 1943

Worked until noon and then I took off for Melbourne, had a date with Betty, went to the show. Saw *The Maltese Falcon,* and had supper and then went to her house. Sure had a nice time.

Wednesday, May 12, 1943

Slept until 1:00 P.M. and cleaned up the cottage. Took island films to be developed and have negatives made and eight sets of pictures made. Also bought a camera, which cost me £8 and 10/s and a calendar for 12/s made of mallee wood. Went to see Fran and went out to supper, had a pretty good time.

Thursday, May 13, 1943

Came back to camp today around noon. Received three letters from the folks. They received the pictures I sent home from the island. Going to bed early tonight and get some sleep.

Friday, May 14, 1943

Well, I worked until noon today and then I took off on liberty. Didn't have a date but I met a very nice girl (blond) by the name of Mavis and I sure had a swell time. Boyles told me not to shove off, but I did just the same.

Saturday, May 15, 1943

Well, I left Mavis at 4:00 P.M. as I had a date with Betty at 4:00 P.M. We went out to supper and then she had to work from 7 to 8:30 P.M. We went to a show and had a bite to eat and I took her home.

Sunday, May 16, 1943

Well, I didn't sleep at the cottage last night, but slept at the YMCA. Then I called up Frances and she asked me to come out. Had supper and went to the Coffee Lounge and then home.

Monday, May 17, 1943

Well, I arrived in camp this morning. I had a letter from Irene and three from Reta in New Zealand. Well, all I can say is that women are slowly driving me mad. Bob and I went to the show in the evening in camp. We saw *Confessions of a Nazi Spy,* which I enjoyed. Also finished taking those pictures.

Tuesday, May 18, 1943

Worked all day long. Received a letter from the folks today. In the evening, I wrote a couple of letters, sent some pictures home and sending some more home tomorrow. Also, signed the payroll. Went to bed early.

Wednesday, May 19, 1943

Worked until noon today. Got paid and then I went into town and I had a date with Norma. Took my films to get them developed. Went out and saw Fran; had a pretty good time. We didn't go out or go any place. I was kind of hard to get along with.

Thursday, May 20, 1943

Went into town. Got a shave, haircut, and face massage. Also got five rolls of film. Going to get six rolls of film Monday. Saw Betty from 2:30 P.M. until 4:30 P.M. Then I called up Fran and went out. We saw *Weekend in Havana*. Went out and had steak and then we went home.

Friday, May 21, 1943

Well, I came back to camp today. I received two letters, one from Margaret Ann and one from Eileen. Stayed in and in the evening, answered some letters.

Saturday, May 22, 1943

Well, I worked until noon and then I took off for Melbourne and went to see Frances. Went to the Coffee Lounge and got the last train back to camp. Also got a picture from Fran.

Sunday, May 23, 1943

Well, worked until noon and then took off for Melbourne. Went and saw Frances and went to the Coffee Lounge again. Had a pretty good time.

Monday, May 24, 1943

Well, I went in and got some films and had some pictures developed, and then I went to see Betty. We went out. She surprised me very much when she said, "You would make a good husband. You're everything a girl could want in a man," and said she "would marry me." Sooooo....

Tuesday, May 25, 1943

Well, I came back to camp today. *Holiday* with Cary Grant and Katherine Hepburn is the picture I saw with Goley and Paul. Got about four letters from Irene today. That's about all.

Wednesday, May 26, 1943

Well, I spent all night in camp. Today I spent the evening writing letters. Oh well, I'll go into town tomorrow. I received three letters from Irene today.

Thursday, May 27, 1943

Well, that was a mistake on my part. No it wasn't. I went into town today and met Betty, we went out and had tea and then went to the show and saw, *For Me and My Gal,* and then I went home.

Friday, May 28, 1943

Well, I saw Betty at 4:00 P.M. I had a date with her for 2:00 P.M. but didn't make it. I saw the picture *First of the Few,* then we ate and she went back to work. I went to the Trocadero and met a girl by the name of Jean Ackley; taking her out Tuesday.

Saturday, May 29, 1943

Well, I came back to camp today. Got four letters from Irene and one from the folks. I stayed in camp and wrote eleven letters. I received the pictures of the folks.

Sunday, May 30, 1943

Worked until noon and then I went into Melbourne and saw Frances. I didn't feel any too good, though. Didn't go any place except out to eat.

Monday, May 31, 1943

Went into Melbourne and had a date with Betty in the afternoon and also in the evening but I got sick in the evening. I think I'm getting malaria.

Tuesday, June 1, 1943

Didn't see Betty at all today as I was feeling pretty sick. Didn't get out of bed until after three. Had a date with Jean. We went to the pictures and saw the picture, *Panama Hattie,* with Red Skelton, and then took her home. Had a good time. She sure is a swell girl, 23 years old. She sure wants my ring bad.

Wednesday, June 2, 1943

Came back to camp and am feeling pretty damn sick. Went to sick bay. They are sending me to the hospital; am standing by for the ambulance. Arrived in the 4th General Hospital at 7:40 P.M.

Thursday, June 3, 1943

Spent the day at the hospital, feeling a little better now. Saw a puppet show here, that's about all. Read two letters from the folks and one from Mrs. Peterson. Called up Jean and talked to her for about ½ hour.

Friday, June 4, 1943

Well, they put me to work today down in the mess hall, but I got peeved and told them where to go and walked out. I called Jean up today and not yesterday and the phone was off and just came on today.

Saturday, June 5, 1943

Worked in the mess hall and dished out breakfast chow and then walked out. Called up Jean and then I wrote a few letters and read some.

Sunday, June 6, 1943

Worked in the mess hall again this morning, but first dished out breakfast. Called up Jean but she wasn't there. Called Frances. That's all.

Monday, June 7, 1943

Well, I wrote Betty a letter and Irene one too. Have my other diary re-copied up to August 3rd of '42 now. Played blackjack last night. I was out 7 ½ £ but came back and ended up 2£ the loser. Some life.

Tuesday, June 8, 1943

Well, of all people, I ran into Bob Berger here in the hospital. Boy it sure was good to see him again. Called up Jean again today, also called Frances and wrote a letter to Betty and one to the folks. Worked in the mess hall again this morning. Also bumped into Tebbe, he's going to get a survey.

Wednesday, June 9, 1943

Well, two of the boys in my ward are leaving. My outfit is out on a 60-mile hike. Have recopied my old diary from June 6, 1942, until August 28, 1942.

Thursday, June 10, 1943

I now have my diary up to August 30, 1942. Well Carl went out today. I saw Davis and visited him in the evening. Called Jean and Frances both on the phone. Read a murder mystery, *A Man Lay Dead,* by Ngaio Marsh. Ward now filled up again. Two more boys came in.

Friday, June 11, 1943

Called Jean up. I saw Davis and we played cards. I drew a couple of pictures. In the evening, we went to the show. We saw *Air Force,* which was a very good picture.

Saturday, June 12, 1943

Drew another picture. Called Jean up. Davis and I fooled around all day. In the evening we went to the show and saw *Palm Beach Story.* Also had a couple of shots; had a pint smuggled in.

Sunday, June 13, 1943

Well, no show today. Oh yes, we rented a radio for our room, that is just till we get out. Called Jean and talked for about 45 minutes. Sure would like liberty.

Monday, June 14, 1943

Frank Miller is also in here with us. Hoff and Pete came up to the hospital to see us. Sure was nice of them. Called Jean but she isn't at work as she has the flu. Wrote a letter to Betty.

Tuesday, June 15, 1943

Called Jean again but she is still absent from work. Saw a picture show, *Northwest Ranger.* Then I was in the craft shop and started making a wallet.

Wednesday, June 16, 1943

Didn't make any calls today. Finished my wallet and started on another one. Frank Miller and Jack Davis and I played cards. Shot the bull with Bob Berger.

Thursday, June 17, 1943

Well, I saw Hedy Lamarr in *White Cargo.* Still have a terrible headache which I have had for three days. Drew a picture and got a haircut.

Friday, June 18, 1943

Nothing much going on today. Well, I finished my second wallet and started a cigarette case. I hope I can finish it.

Saturday, June 19, 1943

Called up Jean today, she was wondering what had happened to me. Went to the show and saw *Holiday Inn;* it sure was a swell picture. Hope to get out soon.

Sunday, June 20, 1943

Well, I'm leaving today. Around 1:30 P.M a truck took us back to camp. Little gave me liberty so I went into town and saw Frances and got the last train back to camp.

Monday, June 21, 1943

Well, I started to work in the butcher shop today. Came into town in the evening. Had a date with Jean and saw *The Major and the Minor*. Took the 5:05 A.M. train to camp.

Tuesday, June 22, 1943

Went into town and arrived there around 4:30 P.M. Went to see Betty then went to eat and met a girl by the name of Ruby. Saw Betty again from 7:00 P.M. to 7:30 P.M. then went to see Ruby. Saw her till 10:00 P.M. and came back into town as I had a date with Betty at 10:50 P.M. Also called up Jean.

Wednesday, June 23, 1943

Well, Davis is back in camp today. I finished work around 10:15 A.M. Did not arrive into camp until around 8:30 A.M. At 12:45, I took off for Melbourne and went out to see Ruby. Stayed until 1:30 A.M. and then went into town.

Thursday, June 24, 1943

Got my pants fixed and my overcoat pleated and pressed. Going to go and see Betty today. Saw the show *To Be or Not To Be*. Then I took her home. Had a very nice time.

Friday, June 25, 1943

Well I worked pretty hard today. Cut up 225 pounds of beef stew and 16 whole lambs into chops. Wrote six letters and stayed in camp for a change.

Saturday, June 26, 1943

Came into town around noon, called up Frances and went out to see her and stayed there. Had a very nice time.

Sunday, June 27, 1943

Had a date with Jean today. Saw The Shrine of Remembrance. Had supper and then we went to the Coffee Lounge.

Monday, June 28, 1943

Went up to see Betty and went out to her place. Took Betty and her mother out to supper. Picked up my pictures at Kodak's and they turned out swell.

Tuesday, June 29, 1943

Arrived in camp about 6:45 A.M. and went to work around 9:00 A.M. Had a lot of meat to cut. Six pans of stew, four of bacon, and 730 steaks. Then I called Jean up and came into town. Went dancing at the Trocadero and then took her home.

Wednesday, June 30, 1943

Went out with Betty today and had a pretty good time. We went to the pictures and then had something to eat and then I took her home.

Thursday, July 1, 1943

Went to see Frances and we didn't do much or go any place except to go out and eat.

Friday, July 2, 1943

Went into town with the boys and got pretty well geared up. Went to Navaniter, met Lorraine. Later met a nice WAF, then around 9:30 P.M. I went to the Troc and met Helen and had a swell time.

Saturday, July 3, 1943

Well Frenchy got married today. Oh! Boy, what a day. Took Betty but don't remember what happened, as I passed out.

Sunday, July 4, 1943

Woke up at the Red Cross today with a big head. Called Jean and we went out. I got the 11:33 P.M. train back to camp.

Monday, July 5, 1943

Saw Betty but she was busy so I went to the Troc and had a pretty good time. After the dance, I got a train back to camp.

Tuesday, July 6, 1943

Well, I saw Jean today and we went to the show. Saw *A Gentleman after Dark.* Then we had something to eat and then I took her home.

Wednesday, July 7, 1943

Had a date with Helen but she stood me up, or as the Aussies say, she famed me. I met another girl and we went to the show and saw *Road to Morocco,* which was very good.

Thursday, July 8, 1943

Had a date with Lorraine today. Met her at 9:30 and we went to her place. She sure is a sweet kid and I really enjoyed myself. Left around 12:15 P.M., met a girl by the name of Polly around 1:00 P.M. and left her at 6:20 A.M. to go back to camp.

Friday, July 9, 1943

Well, I got restricted today for coming in late and not having the meat cut up. I don't know for how long, but just the same, it isn't any good.

Saturday, July 10, 1943

Well, it sure seems funny to have to stay in camp and not be able to go out. The boys and I got some beer and they really got me shot, and I mean shot!

Sunday, July 11, 1943

Gee, it sure is a nice day to be out of camp and here I am. Oh well, it can't last forever, I hope, as I sure do miss going out.

Monday, July 12, 1943

I didn't get into town Monday as I didn't get my liberty pass back until Tuesday. I stayed in camp and wrote letters.

Tuesday, July 13, 1943

Well, I went and saw Betty today but she was busy. She thought I was back in the hospital again. I called Jean up and we went to the pictures. She sure was glad to see me again. Got the last train back to camp.

Wednesday, July 14, 1943

Well, I called Frances up and told her I had been on restriction and just got off and went up to see her. Before I went out, I stopped to see Betty. Supposed to drop in and see her Friday as she is quitting her job.

Thursday, July 15, 1943

Well, I went out with Jeanne. In fact, I met her down at the Troc. We didn't get on so well. I didn't take her as I didn't think I would have time and I was a bit wild with her.

Friday, July 16, 1943

Went into town with Ski; started out around 2:00 P.M. and arrived around 7:30 P.M. and pretty well loaded at that. I met a girl by the name of Mary and we had a pretty good time. Have a date with her for tomorrow night.

Saturday, July 17, 1943

Well, I went to see Mary but she wasn't feeling very well so I left around 9:30 P.M. and went down to the Troc. Saw Jeanne, she said she was sorry and asked for another chance. So I got easy, going to see her Tuesday or Wednesday.

Sunday, July 18, 1943

Well, I left camp again today for liberty and went in and saw Frances. She gave me a gold chain for my New Zealand penny. We went to the Coffee Lounge and I really enjoyed myself.

Monday, July 19, 1943

Came back to camp on the 6:30 A.M. train. Took a Jap souvenir over and got them registered and sent home. Then I wrote some letters. In the evening, I went into Melbourne. I saw Betty but for the last time. So ends that chapter in the life of Merle Fisher. Went to the Troc and met a girl by the name of Dot. Have a date for Wednesday.

Tuesday, July 20, 1943

Well, I went in and saw Jeanne but I got peeved and walked off and left her. Then I went down to the Troc. I met a girl by the name of Kathleen. I have a date with her for Saturday night.

Wednesday, July 21, 1943

Well, I went into town and Dot didn't show up so I went down to the Troc. Didn't do so hot and I left by myself.

Thursday, July 22, 1943

Well, I went to the Troc again. It was much better this time. I met a girl by the name of Joyce and we really did go to town dancing. And I mean go to town. I guess I'll see her Tuesday.

Friday, July 23, 1943

Well, I had a date with the girl on the train from Mornington, but she didn't show up either, so I went to the pictures and then back to camp and finally got some rest.

Saturday, July 24, 1943

Well, my date Kathleen didn't show up so I went to the Troc. I saw her there and also Dot, both explained. Dated Kathleen for Sunday and Dot for Monday.

Sunday, July 25, 1943

Well, I overslept and missed my date with Kathleen, so I called up Joyce and went out to see her. Had tea there and also spent the evening there. I had a pretty good time.

Monday, July 26, 1943

Well, I went in town and met Dot. This time she showed up and we had a pretty good time. Went to the pictures and then I took her home. In fact, I think I'll see an awful lot more of Dot that is if it's okay with her, for Thursday night.

Tuesday, July 27, 1943

Well, I went into town again tonight. I went down to the Troc and I saw Kathleen and I took her home. Had a pretty good time. The weather is pretty cold and raining all the time.

Wednesday, July 28, 1943

Well, I stayed in camp. Not that I wanted to, but because I had to as we had to get ready for the inspection tomorrow by our new general, General Sheppard.

Thursday, July 29, 1943

Well, the inspection went off good. He was pretty well satisfied with it too. I went into town but Dot didn't show up, so I went to the Troc. I saw a few girls I know but didn't go home with any of them. It hailed here today, and I really mean hailed. It sounded like it was going to come right through this tin roof.

Friday, July 30, 1943

Well, into town and down to the Troc. I saw Kathleen and also Jeanne. I danced with Jeanne but went home with Kathleen. Saw quite a few girls I know down there but the weather was terrible.

Saturday, July 31, 1943

Same thing; to the Troc and down there I saw Kathleen again, but I didn't go home with her. Met another girl by the name of Peggy and went to the Coffee Lounge. Then I took her home and left her around 5:15 A.M.

Sunday, August 1, 1943

Well, I had a date with Kathleen for 2:30 P.M. but I didn't get in till around 8:45 P.M. so I went to the Palm Grove at 9:20 and left at 10:30 P.M. and came back to camp.

Monday, August 2, 1943

Well, I went into town and I met Peggy. We went to the show and saw *The Falcon's Brother,* and then I took her home and left her at about 4:45 A.M. and missed the 5:05 A.M. train, so I got the 6:30 A.M. back to camp.

Tuesday, August 3, 1943

Went into town and I saw Jeanne and made a date with her for Friday. Met Frank and we went to the Troc. Didn't do any good there though. Went up to the Blue Lagoon from 11:00 P.M. till 1:00 A.M. closing time. Met Phyllis, ate and took her home. Made a date for Sunday at the Ding Out for 7:30 P.M. Also saw Lorraine. Date with her for Saturday.

Wednesday, August 4, 1943

Well, I had a date with Beryll but she couldn't make it so she sent me a telegram. So I stayed in camp for a change. Sure am dead on my feet. It's colder than hell and hailing like I don't know what. Glad she broke the date as I didn't feel like going out.

Thursday, August 5, 1943

Had a date with Peggy. But on the way in I stopped with the boys and did I get stinko. I was really blind. Peggy took me home cause she figured I had too much to drink and go out.

Friday, August 6, 1943

Well, it really happened. I finally took Jeanne out again. We went to the show and saw *The Road to Morocco.* But as I had seen it, I went to sleep to catch up on some I missed.

Saturday, August 7, 1943

Had a date with Lorraine, but she didn't show up so I went to the Troc. There I saw Kathleen and told her how come I didn't meet her. Took her home and made a date for Wednesday.

Sunday, August 8, 1943

Well, I didn't get into town until quite late so I called up Fran. I went out there. We didn't go any place as per usual so I passed the evening there.

Monday, August 9, 1943

Well, I got detached to Camp Robinson today. In the city, I had a date with Peggy, but she took me home as liberty here is up at 1:00 A.M. I got back to camp in time though. I can't see getting back at 1:00 A.M.

Tuesday, August 10, 1943

Roll call at 6:00 A.M.; have to answer it and get in line for chow. First day to work. Boned out two forequarters and one hind in the morning and two forequarters in the afternoon. Had a date with Jeanne after noon. Got back to camp around 11:30 P.M.

Wednesday, August 11, 1943

Well, I did four forequarters in the morning. Getting better. Of course, practice makes perfect. In the evening, I had a date with Kathleen. We went to the show and saw *To Be or Not To Be*. Took her home and came back to camp in time.

Thursday, August 12, 1943

Got through work at 2:00 P.M. Picked up my name stamp and then I went out to see Peggy as I had a date with her. One thing, we don't eat dinner in camp, but at an Air Force place. Linen on the table and swell food. Just like eating in a swell restaurant.

Friday, August 13, 1943

Had a date with Lorraine. Went to Carrum with her as she was in a stage show there. Then came back to town. Got something to eat and came back to camp. Didn't even have time to take her home.

Saturday, August 14, 1943

Well, we got off at noon today till 6:00 A.M. Monday morning. Had a date with Peggy, went to the Troc and then I took her home. Stayed till about 4:15 A.M. Got a bus and went up to the Red Cross.

Sunday, August 15, 1943

Woke up too late to meet Peggy so I went to Palm Grove and met her there. We went home for tea. Met her daughter, Helen. Left early and came back to camp.

Monday, August 16, 1943

Had a date with Lorraine but she had to leave me at 7:30 so then I called up Frances and went out there. Didn't stay long; left at 11:00 P.M. and came back to camp.

Tuesday, August 17, 1943

Had a date with Jeanne. We went to the pictures. We saw *Take a Letter, Darling,* which was very good. Then I took her home. She asked me to go with just her but I told her no. I guess we get paid Friday. I sure hope so, as I can always use money.

Wednesday, August 18, 1943

Well, the 3rd battalion 1st Marines M Company lost four men on maneuvers the other night. Three were killed right away and one died on the operating table and around 12 wounded when some 81 millimeter trench mortar shells fell short. Have a date with Peggy tonight at 7:30 P.M. Get paid tomorrow. So I don't go to work tomorrow, as I have to go to Balcombe.

Thursday, August 19, 1943

Well, I didn't go to work today as I had to go out to get paid. Had a date with Kathleen. We went to the pictures, had a pretty good time. Sent home about 19 pictures of Australia.

Friday, August 20, 1943

Well, I had to work today as the other boys went out to get paid. In the evening I had a date with Lorraine. We went to the pictures and saw *Jungle Book.*

Saturday, August 21, 1943

Well, I went out to the races today for the first time at Flemington. I lost around £3 on the horses. In the evening, I had a date with Peggy, but we didn't go out; we went home instead.

Sunday, August 22, 1943

Well, I went out to see Peggy again. Stayed there and didn't even go anyplace. I took a few pictures of her sister, husband, and the kids. Left early and came back to camp.

Monday, August 23, 1943

Had a date with Kathleen but she didn't show up. I went to the Troc and met Mavis again and dated her for Thursday and also met another girl by the name of Mary Martin. Have a date with her for Wednesday.

Tuesday, August 24, 1943

Well I had a date with Peggy. We didn't go out, just went over to see her brother and his wife. She's going home for about a week or so. I won't see her for awhile. At least she doesn't cost me much.

Wednesday, August 25, 1943

Well, I had a date with Ruth. Went to dinner and then I left her and went out to see Peggy and stayed until 11:30 P.M. as I had to get back to camp.

Thursday, August 26, 1943

Had a date with Mavis but she didn't show up, so I went to the Troc and I really enjoyed myself. After the dance, I went back to camp.

Friday, August 27, 1943

Had a date with Ruth but she showed up and couldn't make it so I went to the Troc and saw Jeanne there and took her home.

Saturday, August 28, 1943

Well, I didn't go to the races today or this weekend. I went out and had a few drinks. In face, quite a few. Had a date with some girl by the name of Nita.

Sunday, August 29, 1943

Didn't wake up until 4:00 P.M., then I got cleaned up and went out and saw Peggy. We didn't go out but I really enjoyed myself. Got back to camp just in time.

Monday, August 30, 1943

Liberty was up at 6:00 A.M. this morning. I got in about 10 to 6, and then by cab. No liberty tonight for anyone. I fell asleep at 5:00 P.M. and didn't wake up again. I really gave my thumb a nice cut at work today.

Tuesday, August 31, 1943

Supposed to go to sick bay at 8:00 A.M. this morning, but went back to bed and woke up at 11:15 A.M., so naturally I didn't work in the morning. Didn't catch hell though, I got out of it. In the evening, I saw the show *Cash and Carry.*

Wednesday, September 1, 1943

Had a date with Kathleen. We went to the show and saw *The Invisible Agent,* which was a fairly good picture. Then we went home as usual.

Thursday, September 2, 1943

Well, I went to see Gwen, whom I met last February, then I called Jean up and took her out. We saw *Between Us Girls,* which was a fairly good picture. So ends one more day for Uncle Sam and one less for me.

Friday, September 3, 1943

Well, no work as I had to go to Balcombe to get paid. Drew £15. B Company had a party for just the original bunch that was on the island. Cost £1 (3.25) per couple. Met a girl by the name of Joyce and took her. I really had a swell time. Got back to camp at 6:30 A.M.

Saturday, September 4, 1943

Well, I'm taking off for the weekend. I have a date with Carol at 5:00 P.M. She didn't show up so I took a run out to see Peggy. They asked me to stay all night, so I did. Didn't go out though.

Sunday, September 5, 1943

Peggy and I took Helen to her aunt's then we went to St. Kilda and ate. I paid the rent and got my mail. Then we went home to eat. I left around 12:30 A.M. and back to camp.

Monday, September 6, 1943

Had a talk on malaria and on leaving and not talking about it here in Melbourne. Went to see Peggy. Bill was there; I left. Went to the Troc, saw Carol there and took her home and came back to camp. Going back to Balcombe tomorrow. Be leaving soon, I guess.

Tuesday, September 7, 1943

Well, I went back to Balcombe and got there at noon and went on watch right away but I didn't mind as I get off tomorrow at noon. Stayed in camp and wrote six letters. Quite an uneventful evening.

Wednesday, September 8, 1943

Woke up this morning sick as a dog. Had an attack of malaria. Didn't turn in or didn't work. At noon I came into town, went to see Peggy. I was put to bed and well taken care of. Bill came up and they went out.

Thursday, September 9, 1943

Peggy took care of me all day long. Around 4:00 P.M., I got up; around 7:30 P.M., I shoved off as she was going to meet Hansel. I got in town around 8:00 P.M. and took a cab out to Carol's house. Didn't stay very late as I left at 11:00 P.M. Went back to town to the Red Cross and went to bed.

Friday, September 10, 1943

Well, I stayed at the Red Cross, had breakfast, and then went back to camp. Going to get off tomorrow at noon. Sent Peggy a telegram. Worked till 8:00 P.M. The boys all got drunk. I had two drinks. Boys said I had gone religious but I still didn't drink.

Saturday, September 11, 1943

Worked till noon then I took off for Melbourne. Went out to see Peggy. Raining. Sure is nasty weather. We didn't go out any place. Left early, around 11:20 P.M. Went back to town to the Red Cross and went to bed.

Sunday, September 12, 1943

Went out to see Peggy. She wasn't feeling very well. It rained all day long so we didn't go out. I left around 9:30 and shoved off, was kinda peeved.

Monday, September 13, 1943

Well, I came back to camp this morning, got a few letters. Got one back I sent to Mike, marked, "Missing in Action." Also got a telegram from Peggy breaking date for Tuesday.

Tuesday, September 14, 1943

Went in town at noon, saw an hour newsreel. Had supper and went out to see Carol. Then I met Mavis. Met Carol at 7:30 P.M. Went to the show and saw *Seven Sweethearts*. Took her home and went up to the Red Cross.

Wednesday, September 15, 1943

Came back to camp at noon. C Company is restricted, will be leaving soon, very soon. Unpacked my sea bag, marked my gear, and got ready in general. Boles went back to his outfit.

Thursday, September 16, 1943

Well, I worked till noon today and then I took off for Melbourne. Went out to see Peggy. We went into town and had supper and went to a show and saw *Keeper of the Flame,* and took her home. Stayed all night. Had a very nice time. I didn't stay with her though. Received a wallet from Reta for my birthday today.

Friday, September 17, 1943

Left on 8:30 train and I got the 9:00 A.M. express back to camp. C Company is leaving in the morning. Wrote a letter to the folks, Irene, and Margaret Ann. Didn't go out, stayed in camp. Fixing up things so when the word comes, I'll be ready. Sent home pictures, wallet, wrist watch, cigarette case, and go to bed. Going to go and see Peggy tomorrow.

Saturday, September 18, 1943

Got off at noon today and went in to see Peggy. I got a little extra time off. It was Helen's birthday. Peggy's sister, Margaret, was in town. We went to the pictures and then we came home and I stayed so I don't go back till Monday morning.

Sunday, September 19, 1943

Well, Peggy, Margaret, and I went to the zoo today and had dinner in town and took Margaret to the station. Then we went home. I left around 1:45 A.M. and went up to the Red Cross to get a couple of hours sleep.

Monday, September 20, 1943

Caught the 5:00 A.M. train from Melbourne back to camp. A lot of C Company went aboard ship yesterday. Donley went over the hill. Took off at noon and went to see Peggy. She wasn't home, she was out with Hansel. She came home shortly afterwards. We didn't go out in the evening. Peggy and I had quite a disagreement. She asked me to stay and everything turned out OK. Although things nearly ended.

Tuesday, September 21, 1943

Well, I got up at 8:00 A.M. Peggy got my breakfast. I left at 9:00 A.M. and went to the city to get the 9:00 A.M. train to camp. Of all people, I saw Lorna at the station. She asked me to see her on my next liberty. At camp, a sergeant from the 5th Marine's Division Intelligence is in the brig. A Jap spy. 7th Marines and Amphibian held back from sailing. A Company going to board their ship in the morning. Received mail from Al, Irene, Reta, Eileen, and a card from Mother.

Wednesday, September 22, 1943

Got off at noon today and went in to see Peggy. She was out with Bill so I shoved off. I went to the Troc and met another Peggy. I was pretty high and we went to the show. Saw *Orchestra Wives,* and took her home. Got the 5:00 A.M. train back to camp.

Thursday, September 23, 1943

Well, back to camp and back to the old grind again. I received a telegram from Peggy around 9:30 A.M. so I shoved off and went out to see her. Bill came out, we went in town. I got the train before him and think I'll forget it all.

Friday, September 24, 1943

Got off at noon, went to Peggy and got my shirt. She had tickets for the show and asked me if I would take her. Went to town and had supper and went to the show and came home. She wasn't feeling very good. I stayed there for the night.

Saturday, September 25, 1943

Peggy got my breakfast with Fran's help, got the 9:15 train and came back to camp. A Company leaving in the morning. Bill got drunk and Teddy beat him up, then Jim beat him up. He has a broken thumb. What a time and what a mess our hut is.

Sunday, September 26, 1943

Well, A Company left this morning along with Signal Company and Medical Company. I got off at noon and went into town to see Peggy. Went to the museum and tea and then home.

Monday, September 27, 1943

Left Peggy this morning and went back to camp. Collins came back to work. He let me off as I had the weekend. So I went back to see Peggy. We didn't go out in the evening but just stayed home.

Tuesday, September 28, 1943

Well, I had to go back to camp this morning but just to report. Then I came back after Peggy. We went to the pictures and saw *Damaged Goods,* which wasn't much and came back home.

Wednesday, September 29, 1943

Well, back to camp and back to work. Just Collins and I working. Leaving 8:00 A.M. in the morning. Collins and I tossed for it. He lost, so I went in to see Peggy. We didn't go out, just stayed home and I got the 11:55 P.M. back to camp.

Thursday, September 30, 1943

Left Balcombe around 9:45 A.M. by truck and went to Camp Murphy. In Camp Murphy around 1 ½ hours and took off on liberty. Went to see Peggy. We went to the pictures and saw *Reunion in France,* and came out and had supper. Then we went to see *Meet John Doe,* and then I took her home.

Friday, October 1, 1943

Well, I took off on liberty around 8:30 A.M. as I couldn't see staying in camp. Went to the show and saw *Five Graves to Cairo,* and ate and went to see *This Above All,* and then I went out to see Peggy. We didn't go out but just stayed home. Got mail, three letters, Mother, Dad, and Jeanne.

Saturday, October 2, 1943

Well, I guess this is the last liberty in Melbourne and we go aboard ship tomorrow. Had dinner in town and went to see Peggy. She had the pictures for me. Got back in camp about 11:15 P.M.

Chapter 3

Destination New Guinea 8

Sunday, October 3, 1943

Well, we're standing by ready to go. It's now 2:30 P.M. and we are aboard train. 2:45 P.M. we left and went to the docks and boarded ship. Pulled out in the bay and anchored. Suppose we will shove out to sea in the morning. Played Marine Corps Hymn as we pulled out.

Monday, October 4, 1943

Well, around 5:30 A.M., we pulled up anchor and set sail???? Got through work around 10:00 A.M., as we only have two meals a day. 9:00 A.M. and supper at 4:00 P.M. Played cards last night and lost £2 10/s or $8.54 American money. Played this afternoon and won 8/s. Played after supper and won 10/s, makes 18/s back. Still out 32/s. Discharged two depth charges early this morning. Two planes escorting us overhead and two cans. Saw porpoises playing in the afternoon. Coast can be seen in the distance as I guess we're going North up the coast. Also got a life belt.

Tuesday, October 5, 1943

Well, second day out at sea. Went on watch at 10:00 A.M. Played cards, lost around 12/s, was out 4; but I made a comeback. Started serving dehydrated potatoes, also used the last of the fresh bread. Weather is kind of cool, water getting rough. Now 7:00 P.M. and getting dark. Starting to get quite windy. Guess we will be in for a storm tonight. Earl Rowe is on the ship and so is Harry Wisner. Last night plane dropped a few flares and a few depth charges were dropped. Had gin and beer. Had three quarts of gin and two quarts of beer and one quart of ale.

Wednesday, October 6, 1943

Third day out at sea. Got off watch at 10:00 A.M. Played a little cards, lost a little money. One plane with us night and day. Weather is swell, nice warm day. Ocean pretty quiet. Had a bottle of beer among the three of us. Around 1:00 P.M., we saw a shark about 50 yards off the starboard side. Played cards in the evening from 3:00 P.M. till 11:30 P.M. Played blackjack, it sure was a rugged game. I lost $90.00. Cleaned me out with the exception of a $1.00. Got reading material and map on New Britain.

Thursday, October 7, 1943

Around 11:00 P.M. last night, they dropped another depth charge. I guess that sub is still after us. Weather is a little cool and cloudy. At 4:00 P.M. we're supposed to be up as high as Brisbane. Well, we didn't get to Brisbane as we expected. Collins played cards, started on $300.00 and went up to £60. We got a little red today although it was mostly windburn. Starting to lose our bar-room tan. Had another bottle of beer. Caught a hell of a cold. This liberty ship is the USS *John Hugg*. Liberty ship and no liberties. Beats me. Can't see it.

Friday, October 8, 1943

Well, they're going to take up mail today. I might go off at Townsville. So far we don't know where we're going to change ships. But we will board a transport. Had an alert around 10:00 A.M. but nothing happened. Borrowed £2 from Collins, lost it in a blackjack game. Sent six letters, one to Peggy. Supposed to hit some port tomorrow. Weather was nice and ocean calm. Cold is worse, sure feel miserable. News over radio yesterday, ships sunk on same course we're on. We're looking out for survivors.

Saturday, October 9, 1943

Weather is swell and warm. Getting sunburned on deck. Passed a couple of big oil patches. Passed Brisbane around 1:00 P.M. yesterday afternoon. Monday we're supposed to be in Townsville. Now we're in the Great Barrier Reef in the Coral Sea. Passed a small island at 5:00 P.M. Destroyers left us at 5:30 P.M.

Sunday, October 10, 1943

Just one week now we've been aboard ship. Truly a beautiful day in the Great Barrier Reefs. Now passed several large islands. Through glasses it looks very bare and desolate and devoid of life. Barren volcanic matter jutting above the sea. Water is a beautiful light blue studded with darker streaks when it is shallow and full of reefs.

Monday, October 11, 1943

Passed a very large oil spot and also an oil tanker quite a ways off on the port side. Mainland can be made out very dimly in the distance. Passed two ships, one ran aground that had been torpedoed; the other ship was salvaging the guns, etc. 9:30 A.M. we dropped anchor at Townsville. Quite a congregation of ships here, 24 all told including a hospital ship. Weather is terribly hot. We don't get off here. Getting tanner every day. Read *Ginkgo Tree,* pretty good book. Can't be much longer before we hit. Naval gunfire late in the afternoon but received no reports on it. Funny not to have a blackout.

Tuesday, October 12, 1943

Late last night for the first time, I saw a large sea snake about four foot long, six inches thick. Morale is very high. Boys quite anxious to get back in action. Weather still nice and hot. Mainland looks pretty nice on the other side. Very rugged looking. No beach, high rocky cliffs dotted with shrub which has the appearance of our fir trees. Around 5:30 P.M. we pulled up anchor and left Townsville. Took on food in the afternoon. Still don't know where in the hell we are going. Red Cross contributed candy to be given to the boys along with some newspapers.

Wednesday, October 13, 1943

Today there is the regular two other liberty ships besides ours. But our escort is much more improved seeing as we are in dangerous waters. Six cans now instead of three. Well, I'm another year older now. Gun practice began with .50 caliber and 20 millimeter anti-aircraft guns and the pom-pom sounds like old times. Collins came down with malaria today. Well, today I finally got my short haircut, but definitely! But it sure does feel a 100% better. Nice and cool now. They say we will be there Friday, wherever "there" is. Wrote two letters to Irene yesterday. From tomorrow on, we can expect anything, we're told.

Thursday, October 14, 1943

Well, it's Collins' son's birthday today. Getting burned more every day. Have a nice tan on my arms and shoulders. Late in the afternoon, it rained quite a bit off and on. A notice was posted that a terrific air raid was made on Rabaul. One hundred seventy-seven planes destroyed and 53 ships sunk and 23 barges and seven converted ships of about 1,000 tons.

Friday, October 15, 1943

Around 7:00 A.M., I got up and was surprised to see an island close by on the starboard side and what looked like a mainland on the port side. Some say it is the tip of New Guinea, but don't know yet as we've had no official dope yet. Well, at 3:30 P.M. we're supposed to dock up at Goodenough Island. At 3:20 P.M., we ran aground. 6:15 P.M. we left our ship and went aboard a boat then we proceeded aboard the other liberty ship which was docked up, and then down to the dock. Now at 8:30 P.M. and still on the dock.

Saturday, October 16, 1943

Slept on the dock all night. Did I say slept? Got to bed around 12 P.M. Around 4:00 A.M. I awoke soaking wet, as there wasn't any shelter, we remained so. Our camp was 15 miles away. Did I say camp? We arrived at appointed area, grass six foot tall. Rained all day, everything soaked. Received mail.

Sunday, October 17, 1943

Saw a flying squirrel and also killed a snake. Morning started out hotter than hell. Got the word we can write and say, "On friendly island in the Southwest Pacific." Took roll of film, one of a native. Took a bath twice in small stream behind galley.

Monday, October 18, 1943

Going to set up another galley five miles from here. Praying mantis were seen by me for the first time. Like a grasshopper only about three times as big. Supposed to be here until November 10th. Getting a beautiful tan. Talked to a couple of natives today. Have to wear shirt and hat and long pants, if caught otherwise, $25.00 fine. Enforced by malaria control board. Also, water in the stream is not to be put in ears or mouth on account of black fever. Also got some U.S. airmail stamps. Wrote to Irene, Reta, and Tebbe. At night, LaGasse played the mouth organ and we all really enjoyed it.

Tuesday, October 19, 1943

Well, at 8:30 A.M., Collins, Miller, and I started to go partway up to the waterfall which can be seen from camp. We got back to camp at 12:45. Falls were beautiful, when we reached the top of the first one, two more could be seen directly above it. We really had some tough going through jungle, it was so dense in some places, we had to crawl on our hands and knees to get through. Hope that it wasn't all in vain. Fell about 20 feet but caught myself on a few roots so I didn't go the rest of the way. Of course, if I hadn't, I wouldn't be writing this. My let got cut and my leg got bruised up quite a bit but I guess I was pretty lucky.

Wednesday, October 20, 1943

Well, I got a letter from Reta last night. No mail today. Censorship strict; can't say we left Australia or anything outside of well, happy, or in love. Also received word we will be here from six to nine months and use it as an operational base. Hit and then come back here. 1st Platoon leaving tomorrow for five-day maneuvers. Fixed up our tent pretty good; put white sand in for floor, built a couple of desks and made a box with shelves for our stuff.

Thursday, October 21, 1943

1st Platoon went down to the docks to load up. They're shoving off tomorrow. C Company with the 7th Marines is supposed to have had a couple of heavy bombings. Orders were to dig foxholes today as there has been a lot of air activity. Jap planes have been trying to get in here for the last three days but haven't been able to make it, thanks to our pilots. But it would be nice to break the monotony. Washed my pack for the first time since getting here.

Friday, October 22, 1943

Drew a couple of small pictures. Collins and Miller went down to the tractor park to set up a galley down there. H & S is supposed to come in tomorrow and the rest of B Company is supposed to come in Sunday. LaGasse and I went to the movies in the evening and saw *Ten Gentlemen from West Point,* which was very good. Had mail call, I received one letter and it was from the folks. Also, we drew fresh eggs, butter, and apples.

Saturday, October 23, 1943

Well, the 2nd Platoon shoved off today for their five days of maneuvers. Lane and I washed pots and pans as we have no mess men. Wrote a letter to the folks. Well, we actually had an air raid this morning. One Zero came over but only dropped one egg. He tried to get one of the ships but he missed it. The 1st Platoon came back today. They went to New Guinea. Some brought back some native grass skirts. Wrote Carol a letter. We killed another snake about four feet long. Had cookies and pie today which we baked.

Sunday, October 24, 1943

Well, J. B. is back with us. H & S Company came in around 9:00 A.M. We had to get up at 4:00 A.M. and make coffee for the working parties. Charlie, Walt, Pete Woreley, Teddy, J.B., and Boyles came in with H & S. Also the rest of B Company came in. In the evening we went to the show and saw *Pacific Passage,* with Mary Astor and Humphrey Bogart.

Monday, October 25, 1943

Well, to start the morning off at around 11:00 A.M., we had an air raid, but it was just one lone Zero. Now they want us to move our camp, so I guess tomorrow we will move. Received a letter from the folks. They received my billfold and cigarette case and pictures. Wrote a letter to the folks.

Tuesday, October 26, 1943

Had an air raid at 5:30 A.M. this morning but didn't anything come of it. H & S started moving. We're going to move if they get all moved. Well, we're still here at camp. I guess we will move tomorrow. Had a bottle of beer tonight.

Wednesday, October 27, 1943

Well, we finally started moving around 8:30 A.M. Finished around 12:30 P.M. I dug up some pieces of pottery. Natives about 500 yards from us, but it's off limits to us. Had an air raid around 3:00 P.M. Sounded good to hear the old machine guns firing again. Lieutenant Bladdi talked to Lane and told him he was going to take me on the blitz as I had asked him if I could go. Sounds like we're going in about three weeks.

Thursday, October 28, 1943

Well, we worked like hell all day long. Boy, this heat is really a killer over here. Dug some more pottery today. Mail came today but I still didn't get any. We had a couple of bottles of beer today. Natives in village took off, said they'll come back after we leave. Start our galley tomorrow with breakfast.

Friday, October 29, 1943

Started our galley with breakfast. Our planes, Liberators (40), went on a raid to Rabaul. A P-38 came in with one motor dead.

Saturday, October 30, 1943

Got some PX supplies on the cuff. Cigarettes, razor blades, toothbrush, tooth powder, soap, and stationery. Lieutenant Bailey said he will try to fix up my warrant and also try to get me sergeant. A duck came in last night and took off this morning. Paul got his ring Thursday. None of us have heard from Australia. I guess we're not on the beam.

Sunday, October 31, 1943

First thing this morning, Paul and I went to the native village. They had two canoes with carvings on the prow. Then we went out to the beach. Saw quite a few starfish. Painted our galley sign, "Pole Cat Inn." Received a letter from Eileen. J.B. got his orders at 8:30 P.M. and got a plane to Milne Bay to join up with A Company.

Monday, November 1, 1943

Well, rained nearly all day. No mail. Went to the movies but the machinery broke down so I didn't see any show.

Tuesday, November 2, 1943

Received a card from Jeanne and Ray. Read *Crime against Society.* 30 Jap bombers tried to get us, but were intercepted. One shot down and the rest took off. 3rd Division U. S. Marines landed near Bougainville and are fighting.

Wednesday, November 3, 1943

Got some clothes, socks, shorts, and dungarees. Worked on Paul's towel. Wrote Jeanne a letter. Mail came in but I still didn't get any. Went to the show and saw *Striped for Action,* which was very good.

Thursday, November 4, 1943

Mail finally got here. I received a letter from Peggy, Irene, and three from Reta, one from Tom, Jeanne, and two from the folks. Wrote to Peggy and to the folks. Fixed up our tent, carried sand for the floor. Had fresh meat. One Marine killed by a python. They got the snake but too late. Saw Bob Hope and Dorothy Lamour in *They Got Me Covered.*

Friday, November 5, 1943

Wrote to Reta, Tom and Jeanne. Went swimming all morning. Heard I'm going up for sergeant. Got issued some scat for protection against mosquitoes. Got paid £10 today. Put £1 in for PX supplies. Rained in late afternoon and didn't let up.

Saturday, November 6, 1943

Letter from Eileen. Helen is going to get a divorce. No mail leaving here next week. Going with 3rd Platoon. Mr. Baily asked the Captain for me. In the evening saw *Washington Slept Here.* Anti-aircraft practice going on all night long.

Sunday, November 7, 1943

Wrote a letter to Reta and squared away a lot of my gear. Mortars and machine guns firing all day long. No mail. Won't be long now. Went to the movies in the evening and saw *In the Valley of the Sun.* Had to walk better than three miles back.

Monday, November 8, 1943

Well, George shipped over. They promised me Chief Cook but found out I'm losing a rank as I'll be made an assistant cook. Went to the movies and saw *Spitfire.*

Tuesday, November 9, 1943

Issued knife and sheath. Slept all afternoon and read *The Glorious Pool,* by Thorne Smith. Which I enjoyed immensely. My ear is coming along much better now. Went to the show and saw Tim Holt in *Bandit Ranger,* and also a comedy with The Three Stooges.

Wednesday, November 10, 1943

Well, today is the Marine Corps' birthday. Drew stores today for 10 days. Saw a wallaby last night. Also saw a large snake about eight feet long believed to have been a python. In the evening, went to the movies and saw *Reveille with Beverly.*

Thursday, November 11, 1943

Well, we got turkey today and I cleaned them. Had turkey for supper. Rained all day long. We made 11 quarts of home brew and two gallons of stump juice. Sure smells good just to let it work for a few days.

Friday, November 12, 1943

No mail. Washed clothes. Got feeling good on our home brew. Went to the show *Edge of Darkness,* with Errol Flynn and Ann Sheridan but we got soaked and then the machine broke so we didn't see it. In the afternoon, I got some schooling on the .30 caliber machine gun. Learned how to field strip one and adjust head space, load, fire, and fix jams.

Saturday, November 13, 1943

Still raining. Made a couple of Christmas cards and finished Paul's towel. Slept all morning. Worked on Paul's towel, made a label for our home brew, "Pole Cat Bitter Beer," "Government Product," "For Consumption Overseas Only." In the evening, saw a stage show by the 1st Marines and saw a show, Laurel & Hardy in *Jitterbugs.*

Sunday, November 14, 1943

Did some exercises climbing rope hand over hand without use of feet. Washed clothes. In the evening, I went to the show and saw *Edge of Darkness.* It sure was a swell picture and I really enjoyed it. Oh yes, made some wine.

Monday, November 15, 1943

Well, this morning Frank and I went out to the beach as our outfit was having anti-aircraft practice. I fired 50 rounds of .50 caliber at a balloon but was a little high. Cleaned and learned how to field strip my M-1. Well, I finally made it up to the top of the rope today. Then I did 25 dips or push-ups and then a little running, then we went swimming. If I keep this up, I'll be a rugged individual. Scuttlebutt is now that we will be here until after Christmas but I hope not. Stayed in camp in the evening.

Tuesday, November 16, 1943

Didn't do much all day long as I was on watch. Drank some home brew and really got booned up. Our outfit had our first movie but I already saw it. Laurel and Hardy in *Jitterbugs.*

Wednesday, November 17, 1943

We have natives working in camp today building a mess hall. They sure are a rugged little bunch of men. They get six pence a day. They earn £9 a year and are taxed £2 a year. Wrote a letter to the folks yesterday. Well, I am now a Field Cook. They busted me to private then made me Assistant Cook for one day and then promoted me to Field Cook. So now I should pull sergeants pay of $96.00 per month. Went to the show and saw *Three Hearts for Julia,* with Ann Sothern and Melvyn Douglas. Received a letter from Reta and a card from good old Tebbe.

Thursday, November 18, 1943

Received some more mail today. Two from Irene, one from Margaret Ann, one from Eileen and a card from Eileen and stationery and soap from Eileen's mother. It rained all afternoon. In the evening, they had a show here, *Three Hearts for Julia,* but as I saw it, I wrote a letter to Irene, Marguerite, and Eileen.

Friday, November 19, 1943

Well, today was just another uneventful day. Laid in the sun for about an hour, exercised, and went swimming and washed clothes. Received Christmas package from Mother; cigarettes, candy and V-mail. Package from Jeanne with cigarettes, candy, and peanuts. A letter from Carol. In the evening I wrote Carol a letter and Freddy played the mouth organ for us.

Saturday, November 20, 1943

Nothing out of the ordinary. Got mail, two letters from Reta, one from Betty Fisher, and two from the folks. Had some wine in the evening, I sure got drunk.

Sunday, November 21, 1943

Well, I worked all day long. Went swimming after chow. In the evening we had a show, *King's Row,* with Ann Sheridan, which was a very good picture. George caught hell from the mess officer.

Monday, November 22, 1943

Well, day off today. I got a haircut. Wrote a letter to Tebbe, Reta, and Jeanne. Bought 10 bob worth of airmail stamps.

Tuesday, November 23, 1943

Well, I worked all day today. Started working on a towel for George today. Weather pretty nice today. Also, 1st Platoon shoved off on maneuvers, for how long I don't know.

Wednesday, November 24, 1943

Worked all day today also. Had a bond drive in the 1st Marine Division. I got one 100, one 50, and one 25 bond which came to the total of $131.25. Then mail came in. I got a letter from Reta, Peggy, and two from Irene. In the evening we saw *Commandos Strike at Dawn,* with Paul Muni.

Thursday, November 25, 1943

Well, today is Thanksgiving. We had one fresh egg apiece for breakfast and fresh roast beef for supper. Received another letter from Reta. Rained all afternoon and evening.

Friday, November 26, 1943

Worked all day today. Finished George's towel and started one for Mother. Rained in the afternoon and evening. Got a letter from Reta and got slightly geared up in the evening on wine.

Saturday, November 27, 1943

Boys have the still in good working order. Ran off some today made from whole wheat, pure like water, but boy, what a kick. In the evening, we saw *Mexican Spitfire, Blessed Event,* also The Three Stooges in *Home from the Front,* and a Porky cartoon. Letter from Reta.

Sunday, November 28, 1943

Well, in the morning, I went down to see the still the boys have set up. In the afternoon, I went down to the 1st Marines and saw Phyllis Brooks, Gary Cooper, Una Merkel, and Edward Acare. Pretty good show but the girls looked like bags and I ain't kidding. Went to bed at 8:30 P.M.

Monday, November 29, 1943

Lepore is going to be evacuated to have his back operated on. Took our size for pants (Army) and shirt as we have to wear khaki and save our dungarees for combat. In the evening, we went to bed early and Freddy played the mouth organ for us.

Tuesday, November 30, 1943

Worked all day today. Collins started work today. Got mail from Frances & Jean in Australia, Reta, one form Jeanne and one from the folks. Went to the show in the evening and saw *Flight for Freedom,* with Fred MacMurray and Rosalind Russell.

Wednesday, December 1, 1943

Well, I went to the dentist this morning. One tooth might have to be refilled or pulled. Got new tractors, "Water Buffalos," today. Had a letter from Mother. In the evening, I did a little work on my towel.

Thursday, December 2, 1943

Worked quite a bit on my towel for Mother. No mail. B Company won the baseball game today. Got issued a bush knife, leggings, and shoes. Might leave Sunday. H & S is getting 75 new men in tomorrow. No mail. Worked on towel some more. Hope to finish it tomorrow.

Friday, December 3, 1943

Worked all day today. Got paid £40, bought three $50.00 war bonds and one $25.00 for the folks for Christmas. Altogether it cost $131.25. B Company played H & S, we won six to nine. I also had a bet but had to give two to one odds. I won 10/s. In the evening we did a show, *Two Yanks in Trinidad,* with Brian Donlevy and Pat O'Brien. Lepal got transferred today as he is getting shipped to the States.

Saturday, December 4, 1943

B Company is now in first place in softball in the division. Still holding a high place in volleyball. At Gilbert Islands, we lost 1,096 dead and 2,680 wounded. It is estimated that 5,700 Japs have been killed. In 16 hours of the bloodiest fighting in the Pacific. We're now on six-hour notice. We had a baseball game after supper. We played B Medical and won with a score of nine to five. In the evening we had a movie, Deanna Durbin in *Mrs. Holiday.*

Sunday, December 5, 1943

Well, I worked all day. I sent my pictures to get developed, six bob per roll. Also got ½ dozen Guadalcanal patches. Sent home the receipts for my bonds. Lot of V-mail came in but I didn't get any, maybe tomorrow as a lot of packages came in. Wrote a letter to Marguerite.

Monday, December 6, 1943

Worked all day as per usual. Mail came in. I received a letter from Peggy and one from Nancy Lou and a package from Irene. Saw J.B. today as A Company has come down from Milne Bay. They're only supposed to be here three days and then take off with 37 tractors and one regiment of Army to take a small island. In the evening we had a show, *Joan of Ozark*. Had a baseball game but it was called on account of rain.

Tuesday, December 7, 1943

Reading the book, *Battle of the Solomons,* by Ira Wolfert. Well, we started packing today and breaking camp. We are now on three-hour notice. It's raining out and very dismal out and thundering as if God is voicing his protest against this war and killing and more to come in this next week. I also received a package from home and a lovely Christmas present from Irene and her picture which made me happy. Scuttlebutt is that we are going to Oro Bay and that part of A Company has shoved off today and will be in combat tomorrow. Funny the thoughts a person gets at a time like this; not fear but bewilderment and wondering, or maybe I should say curiosity, as to what lies in the future for all of us. Cleaned my rifle, oiled and sharpened my bayonet and sheath knife. Hope we will have a chance to get those films before we leave. We also got four bazookas, one to each platoon. Fresh meat, steaks and pork chops, and oranges. The fattening of the calf before the slaughter.

Wednesday, December 8, 1943

Well, we packed all of our galley gear today. Tore down our tent and packed our packs ready to leave on three hours' notice. Received a letter from Irene, Peggy, Eileen, Joan, and the folks. In the evening, I went down to see our Aussie cobers. Rained like hell, flooded the roads. Coming back, a bridge was washed out and the water over our heads, so we had to go across on a cable hand over hand. Was I a sight! Like a drowned rat and all mud, and I thought we had rain in the States!

Thursday, December 9, 1943

Finally stopped raining this morning, also we drew an extra canteen. Wrote a letter to Peggy, Irene, folks, Eileen, and Joan. Washed clothes. Saw J.B., Little, Erlick, and Mitchel. Saw my Aussie cobers and obtained some pictures, or I guess I should say negatives. Still standing by. Didn't work today. Wrote a letter to Peggy in the evening and read the *Reader's Digest*.

Friday, December 10, 1943

Didn't work today. Got in some sack time. Paul Breski and Lane moved down to the docks that's 2nd Platoon with the exception of Lane. They're supposed to leave tomorrow in the afternoon. Collins and I went down to the docks and saw some of the fellows in A Company. Frank and the 1st Platoon is moving down to the docks tomorrow after breakfast. Washed clothes and took a swim in the river.

Saturday, December 11, 1943

Worked till noon and then I moved down to the docks. Lane and Collins left with headquarters at about 5:30 P.M. and boarded a landing ship, tank. We're supposed to leave either tomorrow or the next day. Saw Hurechela and some of the boys in A Company as they are still here.

Sunday, December 12, 1943

Daniel Leman fought last night and won. He is now champ of Goodenough Island. Just after dinner, I was told to get my gear and get aboard a tractor. We broke down but we didn't board ship so we slept on the ground but it was pretty cool all night.

Monday, December 13, 1943

Right after breakfast, we moved to where the other tractors were. There I transferred myself and my gear to another tractor. At 11:00 A.M. I drew C rations for the men. At 3:15 P.M. we were aboard. Told me not to work on this ship, as if I would. 4:00 P.M. we shoved off. Four landing ships, tanks plus one cruiser and two cans.

Tuesday, December 14, 1943

Well, it was hotter than hell last night, didn't get much sleep. Not even enough room to lie down. That's how packed we are. Two meals a day. Had breakfast about 9:00 A.M. Dropped anchor at 9:00 A.M. in Buna will stay here until tonight then we shove off for Finschhafen. Played poker, won £7. Planes joined us at 10:00 A.M. Liberators, 10 with an escort of 12 Lightnings took off. Looks like they mean business, quite a few warships here now! At 6:30 P.M. we were notified that we weren't leaving tonight but tomorrow at 4:00 P.M. Awful hot down below. In a half hour all your clothes are soaking wet including your pants.

Wednesday, December 15, 1943

Rained all night last night and came down through the deck soaking all of us. That's getting to be a habit, waking up all wet. 11:30 A.M. we were all called up on the mat for stolen goods being found in the tractors. In one tractor they found two cases of cigarettes and six cases of chow. Slept aboard ship again. Supposed to be at Finschhafen at 7:00 A.M. tomorrow morning.

Thursday, December 16, 1943

Well, it rained all night and I got soaked again as per usual. Landed at 8:30 P.M. —7:30 to be exact, but an hour before we got off, saw Breski and the 2nd Platoon, Miller and the 1st, Lane, Collins, and Headquarters. Moved up to the 3rd Battalion 1st Marines as I'll take chow down to them. A Company landed with the Army and no casualties. Also, Army and Marines landed on New Britain between Cape Gloucester and Gasmata. We are now 22 miles away from the front lines here in New Guinea.

Friday, December 17, 1943

Well, I now have Freddy here with me. He moved up here with me last night. We got drenched to the skin, clothes, blankets, everything. Then we had to move down to I Battery as we are going to get our chow from them. Cassidy is here, he's from Canton, Ohio. Had two air raids, one in the morning and one around 7:30 P.M. I never had so much rain and had to go through so much mud in my life. Up to your knees. I guess I'll start to mumble in the jungle.

Saturday, December 18, 1943

Well, at 4:00 A.M. we had another air raid but they didn't get through. Wright went to the hospital, 2nd degree burns on his legs. I guess he won't go on the blitz. Wrote a letter to the folks, Irene, and Betty Fisher. Suppose to leave next. Saturday, we're to take the airport. Had an air raid around 10:00 P.M. Nothing new. Shaved, washed clothes. Got a shot of the road which was pretty bad.

Sunday, December 19, 1943

Got issued a jungle hammock and have to turn in our cots and bed rolls. Had another air raid around 3:30 A.M. Jap planes dropped eight eggs. Guess I'll have to start sleeping during the day. Had another air raid around 6:15 P.M. A Company came back from New Britain this morning, they landed with the Army 39th Amphibian. They got credited with two Zeros and three machine gun nests. Only one casualty. Sammy Holcomb, one toe shot off and a couple of slugs in each leg from a Zero strafing. They evacuated him from here by plane this morning. A Company is to follow us five days after we hit first. Phillips got himself a Jap. Wrote a letter to Peggy, one to Reta, and one to Mr. & Mrs. Boehm. Heard the radio with good music from one of the jeeps.

Monday, December 20, 1943

Heard "Amen," "Brazil," etc. last night. No air raid but I woke up at 4:00 A.M. just the same. Freddy LaGasse got transferred to the 2nd Platoon. We are taking five Buffalos from 2nd Platoon on the blitz with us. A Company made the news this morning. Dugout Doug was on Goodenough, some of the boys saw him. Said we may get moved tomorrow.

Tuesday, December 21, 1943

Had an air raid around 9:00 P.M. last night and one from 4:00 until 6:00 A.M. this morning. Rained all night. Roads are awful bad this morning, one of them you can't even get through. Glad it won't be long now, we will go in action this weekend. Heard our band play and put on a little show. Wagner gave me a girl's address in Sydney, his future wife's sister. We're not at Finschhafen but 11 miles down from there, so they say.

Wednesday, December 22, 1943

Had an air raid around 4:00 A.M. again this morning, don't know what time it was over as I went back to sleep. Wrote a letter to Wagner's girl's sister, Raymondi, in Sydney. Got a haircut. Paul brought me up some mail. One from the folks and two letters from Reta in New Zealand. Went to sleep without any air raids.

Thursday, December 23, 1943

Jack showed me the native cemetery which really was a nice thing to see. Hope I get some shots of it. Also read, *The Case of the Stuttering Bishop* and *The Case of the Counterfeit Eye*, by Erle Stanley Gardner. Also read *The Case of the Lucky Legs*. 2nd Platoon went aboard ship. Saw Earl Rowe. Had an air raid around midnight.

Bismarck Operation Begins 9

Friday, December 24, 1943

Had another air raid around 3:00 A.M. this morning. Got orders to pack up my gear and go aboard Doyle's Buffalo. We're to board ship around 11:00 A.M. We go aboard ship tomorrow. Got a Christmas bag from the Red Cross. Had an air raid around 8:30 P.M. I'm going to be ammunitions man for the guns on our tractor.

Saturday, December 25, 1943

Well, we had two air raids this morning before dawn. We'll have dinner and supper and breakfast tomorrow aboard ship and then we hit. General Krueger and General Shepherd are here inspecting ships. Also war correspondents.

Sunday, December 26, 1943

Well, we started working on our tractor at 2:00 A.M. We had breakfast at 5:00 A.M. At 6:00 A.M. we could see all the ships laying down a barrage. We have four cruisers and 28 cans. At around 7:00 A.M. we got some air support; they are Liberators. H hour is 7:45 A.M. we follow 50 minutes after the initial landing. Well, here goes! We got ashore around 9:00 A.M. Sure is rugged country. And boy, hell sure is a popping. Around 2:35 we had some Zeros come in dive bombing and strafing. We lost two planes and got one Zero. Also, they got one of our LSTs. Then Stokeridge, the Hansen twins, Oswald, and an OM man went to clean out two pill boxes. Approximately 68 Japs. OM man got it. One Hansen boy shot in the hand and fell off the tractor. They got him with a hand grenade. Oswald is dead. Bullets and bayonet wounds. The other Hansen is aboard ship. One new crew as we lost one Alligator as both tracks came off. Our Liberators came over around 4:15 P.M. and bombed the hell out of them. I Company 7th Marines got hit pretty heavy. Now to top it off, there's a 5-inch dud about two feet under our tractor. Now we're 800 yards from the front. Guess we'll see all our action tomorrow when we go after pill boxes. Saw General Shepherd here. We're about 30 yards from the beach area, looks like a bit lawn mower cut the trees in half. There's two half-tracks and 55 Sherman tanks within 30 yards of us, plus tractors.

Monday, December 27, 1943

Well, at around 7:00 A.M. we got started and headed down to where we landed. Then we got some troops and were told our objective was the small island. Well, here we go! Just got back. The island was deserted, just empty pill boxes and communications. Boy, we sure went in there firing as we saw the pill boxes as we approached the isle. Came back to our area. Went over that 5-inch dud again, but it didn't go off, thank God! Loaded up with 60 millimeter and 81 millimeter, now we're going to the front. Of all the breaks. We hit a coral reef and lost our tractor, the load, and most of our gear. What we did save is sure a mess.

Tuesday, December 28, 1943

Wringing wet! No dry clothes! No place to sleep! The 12th Defense came in yesterday, also some more LSTs came in. They're nearly up to the fighter strip but things are going pretty tough. Here we go again. The Japs are breaking through behind us. Hope I can write tomorrow!

Wednesday, December 29, 1943

God! What a night in a foxhole, had to stay awake lying in six inches of water, raining all night. Wet, muddy, colder than hell! Still have to keep an outpost. Just at dawn, and before we were relieved, the Japs took a few shots at us but they didn't hit anybody. At 2:30 A.M. we had an air raid. At 5:00 A.M. we were supposed to be attacked but weren't. Planes really giving the Japs hell. Fifty bombers or more were dropping their loads. Here the ground trembled. 5th Marines came in today. K Company and I Company First Marines really caught hell.

Thursday, December 30, 1943

Well, it's still raining. God, what a muddy mess everything is. I'm tired of staying around here, I'm shoving off. Arrived up at the advanced CP around 5:00 P.M. Saw a lot of dead Japs on the way and do they *stink!*

Friday, December 31, 1943

Well, we're moving up to the airport this morning. Got hell for shoving off and moving up near the front. Raining like hell. Don't think the sun ever shines on this island. At least I've haven't got to see it. Saw around five bombers wrecked and a few Zeros. Set up a galley and fed the men. Few snipers in here taking a few shots. Jap planes dropped about eight eggs. What a New Year's Eve.

Saturday, January 1, 1944

Still raining. My gear will never get dried out. I got a Jap bayonet today. Mitchel's here. Also saw Price today. They're operating with a patrol. Got mail. Seven letters; pretty lucky or what!

Sunday, January 2, 1944

Well, today it wasn't raining for a change and I got some of my gear dried out. Erlick came in today. We're going to move about two miles up and set up a beach defense. Around 9:00 P.M., two Jap planes came over and dropped some eggs; only dropped two near us. Sure was a nice sight to see search lights on the planes and tracers going up from the ack-ack gun. Just like old times. I hit the deck so hard, I skinned up my ribs on some branches.

Monday, January 3, 1944

Had another air raid around 3:00 A.M. Woke up and he was overhead, tracers flying all around. I got out of my sack in no time. Saw Val and Davis this morning. Getting ready to move now. Moved down to the new area. Remains of a Jap beach defense and a few wrecked Jap houses. Had two air raids in the evening.

Tuesday, January 4, 1944

Went to the airport today and got a few shots, they should be good. Also some of Jap huts. Started raining like hell and didn't let up. No air raids. We can write now if you can get paper. Say you were in action against the enemy. That's all!

Wednesday, January 5, 1944

Well, H & S came in today I'm sorry to say. I went to the front, got a new Jap helmet, few postcards, and some Jap ditty bags. Clothes, which are pretty nice, one bundle of socks, a jacket, and a raincoat.

Thursday, January 6, 1944

Worked on our galley all day long. Rained like hell all day long. We were supposed to start cooking here today but there was no water available, couldn't even have coffee. Rained all night long as per usual.

Friday, January 7, 1944

Well, we worked all morning long getting stores. Had to carry them quite a ways to the truck as it couldn't get through mud up to my knees. Such rain and mud I've never seen in all my life. Started supper here. Pumped water with a gas-pump by hand; we got 125 gallons. What a hell of a job that was. No air raid; raining like hell, yet.

Saturday, January 8, 1944

Well, I got mail. I got one letter from the folks. Well, it rained again today. What a hell hole this turned out to be. Had an air raid around 4:30 P.M. Another one around 6:00 P.M. Had another around 8:00 P.M. Heard him drop a few then 90s cut loose, tracers flying around all over. Could hear him pretty plain as he was quite low. Had another one a little later on. Condition was red, then green. I went to sleep. They said we had another one around 3:15 A.M. but I was enjoying my sleep.

Sunday, January 9, 1944

Well, I'm on watch. I get off at noon today. Not raining right now but I expect it to some time today. Lane got the word that he's being transferred to the States with Johnny Care from B Company. Cleaned my weapon and what a rusty job. Got mail, one letter from Irene. Sure took a lot of kidding about having my head shaved. Started raining about 7:00 P.M. and did it rain all night long. Had one air raid and that was all. Sent a letter home with Jap newspaper clipping and a few stamps. Just two years ago tonight since I saw Irene last.

Amber flare with parachute, objective taken and landing successful.

Air raid, three repeated times, tank attack.

Secure, four.

Gas, constant ringing of bells.

Emergency, red cartridge

Green star cluster, landing no good, objection not taken.

Fire falling short, white star cluster.

Fire barrage, amber star cluster.

Hitting our own troops, white star parachute.

Present position, green star parachute.

Monday, January 10, 1944

Well, it rained all day long. I wrote a couple of letters, one to Peggy and one to Irene. This is my day off. I went on at noon. We saw about 400 natives go by us. They were up about 10 miles and they made them move so as they wouldn't get killed by the Japs and our shells and bombs. There were quite a few small children and dogs. Old men that couldn't walk, they carried on litters. Had one air raid but nothing happened. I guess they didn't get in.

Tuesday, January 11, 1944

Well, I got Frank to cook dinner for me and I take supper. Bill and I went up to the Jap village again. I got a matchbox from the Philippines, Christmas card, cartoon postcard which I sent home. Yesterday I sent a Jap newspaper clipping and a few stamps. Lane got his LST and left here yesterday for Brisbane. Rained like hell last night and did I get wet. Mail came in, one letter from Jeanne and Ray and one from the folks. Three fellows nearly drowned today but Little pulled two out and somebody else got the third one out. They don't know whether he will live or not. The one fellow did die. Order out; no swimming in the ocean. Well, Breski is back here with us as the 2nd Platoon came back. One air raid around 9:00 P.M.

Wednesday, January 12, 1944

Well, nothing much happened today. Two years in the service today. J.B., Little, Teddy, Pete, Erlick, Miller, Worley, Palermo, and myself all got booned up on 190 proof alcohol. Wrote a letter to the folks. Of course, it rained.

Thursday, January 13, 1944

Well, Frank and I took off and went up to the front. We were gone about six hours. We went through five or six Jap villages but we couldn't find anything worthwhile. I brought back two .47s, some .25s, a few .60 caliber, and a few grenades. Took the .47s apart and dismantled them. Nick took to grenades apart for us. Gee, the fellows sure got nervous when we started dismantling them. Boy, we sure were tired when we got back. Got 250 yards from the front and they wouldn't let us go any further.

Friday, January 14, 1944

Well, I'm off today for a change. Went to the dentist. He didn't pull any, just put some stuff on it and said if it hurt any more to come back and he would pull it. Wrote a letter to the folks, sent them 4 postcards and a picture of a Jap soldier. Made some fudge which turned out pretty good. Said 90 to 80 planes of ours would be over between 8:00 and 9:00 P.M. Shaved my head for the third and last time. No air raids or nothing. Tojo isn't on the ball lately. Still raining.

Saturday, January 15, 1944

Rained like hell last night and still raining. Was going to try to get past the front, but on account of the mud, it would be too hard to get up there and back by noon. Read the book *Roaring Guns,* by Ken Ranger. Saw quite a few natives go by today. Some of them had such sores on them that it nearly made you sick. Announced that 1,320 bags of second class mail was sunk, mostly November mail. Anti-aircraft guns were test firing. Announced that services will be held at the airport in memory of those killed.

Sunday, January 16, 1944

Well, it rained all night again. At around 9:00 A.M. we left camp in the tractors and headed for the airport. Sure did rain, but I didn't mind getting wet on the occasion. The cemetery is on the airport. Seventeen graves there, (U.S.A.F.) U.S. Armed Forces. The ceremony was nice and when they blew that bugle, it was something you won't forget and that really gets you. Guess they're going to dig up the other boys and put them up there too. Still raining like hell. So ends this day.

Monday, January 17, 1944

Well, at 3:00 A.M. this morning we had an air raid. Condition red. Then at about 6:10 A.M. we had another one; you could see flares out at sea as we had some ships coming in that they tried to get. One Jap sniper at 660 killed 21 Marines before they got him. In the evening, Pete, Erlick, Teddy, Miller, Collins, and myself got looped to the gills on 190 proof alcohol. Had two more air raids but had too much to notice them.

Tuesday, January 18, 1944

Well, to start out with, I had a tooth pulled this morning. No dentist chair, so they used the operating table. Heard some bad news; the "Major" Charles Boles in the 7th Marines, our doughnut man at Balcombe, got killed. Also, Eastwood of our outfit in B Company got killed yesterday by shrapnel. So pass away a couple of nice fellows. Both of them were with us on the island. Young Burr cracked up and was evacuated.

Wednesday, January 19, 1944

Well, today was of little importance. We had around five air raids and one around 6:10 A.M. this morning. Read *Trouble Riders* by Max Brand and *The Black Camel,* by Earl Derr Biggers. Rained all day long as is the habit here. So ends another day. Wrote a letter to the folks, sent pictures of Jap woman and double postcard of landing.

Thursday, January 20, 1944

Well, had two air raids this morning; one around 5:30 A.M. and the other a little after 6:00 A.M. Charlie Palermo went to the hospital with 2nd degree burns as a stove blew up. Jack Davis is in the hospital. Scronski, as a tree fell on him when sleeping. They had to cut the tree to get at him. Comtrell is gone as he cracked up. Sent home a package of souvenirs. Stopped raining this afternoon. Read *The Black Camel,* by Earl Derr Biggers, it's a Charlie Chan mystery.

Friday, January 21, 1944

Well, the most unusual has happened. I awoke this morning and found the sun shining brightly. In the morning, anti-artillery guns and machine guns were test firing, sounded like old home week. I read *The Case of the Sulky Girl,* by Erle Stanley Gardner. One important thing that I omitted yesterday; we had fresh meat. Steak for dinner and hamburgers for supper. Dried stuff today but the only thing in the way of meat, corned beef.

Saturday, January 22, 1944

Well, last night we had a couple of air raids. One was right on the ball; 32 guns opened up. Man what a sight; all those tracers going up in the air, but it turned out to be one of our own planes. In the afternoon, I set off with Fadden for the hills. We arrived at the front lines but were not allowed to pass the barbed wire entanglement. We turned about and headed towards Sago. Met the natives as they are camped up there. Spent the remaining hour or so there.

Sunday, January 23, 1944

Received a letter from the folks yesterday. Also read *The Adventures of Sherlock Holmes.* Started reading *The Magnificent Obsession,* by Lloyd D. Douglas. Again we have sunshine today. Also four LSTs came in today. Hope we get mail tonight. No such luck. No mail. Not even an air raid.

Monday, January 24, 1944

Well, no air raid this morning. Sure was a beautiful day again today. In the afternoon I went in the surf in the ocean, boy what fun. I lost my hat as a result. Then I washed clothes, played cards, and also read *The Magnificent Obsession.*

Tuesday, January 25, 1944

Well, I started reading *Topper Takes a Trip.* If these campaigns don't crack me up, Thorne Smith's stories will. Had an air raid around 6:00 A.M. Well, the afternoon was really something. The Captain told us we were going to go back to Guadalcanal and that after we left here, we would no longer belong to the 1st Marine Division but to the 1st Amphibian Corps. Then mail and packages came in. Boy, what a boost in morale. It is impossible for a person to realize that mail can do so much for the fellows out here in the battle zone, or should I say battlefield.

Wednesday, January 26, 1944

In the mail yesterday I received a toilet set from Eileen, a letter and a card from her mother, letters from Peggy, Irene, Norm, a card from Jeanne, and a card from Eldridge. No air raids, but on the whole, it was a rather nice day. Of course it was pretty hot but that's to be expected over here. They just went after more mail! Now they tell us our chances of going home are slimmer, if that is possible. Boy, what a day for mail. I got three from Peggy, John, Jean Oakley, five from the folks, one from Joan, two from New Zealand. Val came up and saw us. I guess they're going to make a push in the next few days at Borgen Bay. Had an air raid about 4:00 P.M. but it didn't last very long and nothing came of it.

Thursday, January 27, 1944

Well, had an air raid this morning around 5:00 A.M. as usual. Then Collins and I went down to C Company to see Val and Davis. On the way down they were dynamiting so we had to stop. I looked up in time to see a big chunk of wood about to descend upon my head and ducked hastily thereby receiving only a glancing blow on the shoulder. In the afternoon we had an air raid in which six Marines lost their lives and two natives were wounded. Also, we received mail, one from Australia and two from the folks. So ends one more day in the Marine Corps.

Friday, January 28, 1944

Well, it started out by raining and an air raid. The day passed quite uneventfully and the biggest part of the afternoon was taken up by writing letters. Mail came in. I received one letter. It was from Betty Fisher and another air raid at supper time and thus another day passes.

Saturday, January 29, 1944

Had an air raid first thing this morning and two more later on in the afternoon. Mail came in. I got a letter from Peggy, and a cake, letter from Reta, Irene, and Mrs. Peterson. Paul Hansen is going home tomorrow and believe me, he sure deserves it after losing one brother in New Georgia in the Amphs., and one here and what he went through. They said his mother will receive the Navy Cross for his brother and he will get the Silver Star.

Sunday, January 30, 1944

Well, it rained almost continuously all day long. Landing ship, tanks came in today. Paul Hansen left here at 8:00 A.M. to go to New Guinea on one. General Shepherd landed on the airfield today. The first planes landed here on Friday, January 28th. Cleaned my rifle. Mail came in on the ships but we won't get it until tomorrow. Wrote the folks, Irene, Mrs. Peterson. At 4:30 P.M. there was a loud explosion at sea which vibrated the ground. Thought it was a depth charge. Then air raid was sounded. We can see the ships getting in battle formation. Hope we see some action!

Monday, January 31, 1944

Well, it rained all day today again. I think I've seen more rain since I've been here than I ever saw in the States all my life. Mail came in. I got two letters and two packages from Reta in New Zealand. Had one air raid was all. Wrote a few letters, one crazy one to Irene.

Tuesday, February 1, 1944

Well, today it's still raining. Ski got a 2nd degree burn. Frank is pretty sick. Surprise! Today we had *ham. Real ham!* I know. I couldn't believe it either. It finally cleared up a little; that is, the sun came out for a short while. Mail came in today but I didn't receive any.

Wednesday, February 2, 1944

Well, it rained all day today as per usual. I don't believe I've ever seen so much rain and mud, especially all in one place and all the time. Had an air raid in the afternoon. The rest of the day was just spent. Played cards in the evening; won three out of five games.

Thursday, February 3, 1944

Rained again today. Not all day. We had a few hours' intervals of nice weather, not nice, but beastly hot. Cleaned my rifle, also made a band for my watch. Had an air raid around 5:00 A.M. this morning. Washed clothes and in the evening we played cards. News this morning, 4th Division Marines and 7th Army hit the Marshall Islands and made 28 landings and 10 beachheads.

Friday, February 4, 1944

Well, it rained nearly all day again today. I read a Western magazine. I drew a new hammock today and put it up. The rope broke and I came down. The boys thought it was funny but I sure didn't. Had an air raid but it only lasted 10 minutes or so. Mail came in today. I got a letter from Reta, Betty, and Mona in Sydney. In the evening we had some more rain.

Saturday, February 5, 1944

Well, it rained like hell this morning again. It's just one continuous rain with brief pauses. Had an air raid again today around 10:15 A.M. but it lasted only a short time. In the afternoon, I wrote a few letters; so passed the afternoon.

Sunday, February 6, 1944

At 1:15 A.M. this morning we had an air raid which was right on the ball. The A.A. fire sure was something to see. Rained again, but not too long. In the afternoon we had another one. Played cards till dark; we won four out of six. Then around 9:30 P.M. we had an air raid. One plane just secured and two more came in from the other side. Talk about A.A. fire! I think it's about the best I've ever seen. Sure is a beautiful sight to see. Sky fairly clear, moon out, searchlights go on, plane is caught in light, A.A. fire lets go, red tracers fill the sky.

Then announcement came over, "Honorable Tojo loose one plane breaking in half." But of course we knew as we saw it. It's just that it was confirmed. Two waves coming in, one 60 miles out, the other one 45 miles. One 45 miles out came in to 2 ½ miles. Three planes then, just one came in but didn't get him. This went on for a few hours; then I fell asleep.

Monday, February 7, 1944

Had one air raid this morning. Taking Alligators aboard LST as we are getting three new types of Buffaloes in. One unarmored, one armored and one armored with turret and a 37 MM in it and three machine guns for assault. Got two bars of face soap and tooth powder, first we have been able to get. Also got four hams. Had creamed ham for supper. Also *fresh eggs,* 1 ½ per man for breakfast tomorrow. Received mail from folks, Betty, Reta, Nana, Lou, Tebbe, and the union.

Tuesday, February 8, 1944

Well, no air raids yet. Raining again as per usual. I'm answering letters now. Tony Boughany, 2nd Class Corpsman in H & S, shipped over to the Marine Corps and made 2nd Lieutenant, is going back to the States to go to Officers Training School. Also, Mac leaving tomorrow, got his rate changed from Platoon Sergeant to Staff Sergeant, He's going into Aviation Photography. Raining and muddy as hell! Mail came in. I got mail from Irene, Jeanne, Myron, Folks. No air raid what-so-ever, it's dead.

Wednesday, February 9, 1944

What a day, raining to beat hell. Tony and Mac left this morning. Made some cheese omelets for breakfast and some dumplings for dinner. In the afternoon it cleared up but it can't last. Answered letters all afternoon and played cards, we won three out of three. Also I got a nice package from Irene. Air raid again, one sneaked in and dropped a couple of them pretty close. These guys are too jumpy. Came in again and dropped six eggs.

Thursday, February 10, 1944

Well of course it rained today. Wrote a few letters today, also sent home that native piece of wood. Poor "Chief" cracked up today. He's as crazy as a bat. Guess it's getting to be too much for the old boys. Have a couple of more fellows that are liable to crack up. Had an air raid, the raider must have been asleep; he came in and dropped two in the bay between here and A Company. Sure could feel the vibration from it. Only two eggs though, came in 9:30 P.M. Played cards and got feeling good. Going to distill some more tomorrow. And another air raid later on and he dropped quite a few eggs.

Friday, February 11, 1944

Well, was another one of those days. In the afternoon I washed my clothes, blanket, towel, etc. Then went swimming in the ocean for awhile. Had fresh meat. Some sausage for breakfast, steak for dinner, and hamburgers for supper.

Read a Western romance. In the evening we played cards. They evacuated "Chief" today. Sure feel sorry for him; he was a nice kid. Four transports flew in today, also four liberty ships which brought us 100 new Buffaloes. Got a letter from the folks last night. Got feeling good on 190 proof alcohol. No air raid. Rained like hell all night.

Saturday, February 12, 1944

No air raid this morning. Raining again today as per usual. We're putting up a tent today as its orders from the Captain. Wrote a letter to the folks and read a Western magazine. In the evening we listened to the radio. Had an air raid but everything was O.K.

Sunday, February 13, 1944

Well, we really had some bad luck. Early this morning we had an air raid. We lost six men: Castro, whose head and abdomen hasn't been found; Overstreet, who was under a tractor which caught on fire, just his abdomen left; Bankoskie; Sergeant Ritter; Graham; Blair; also Carmichael who died later on.

1. Tucker—?
2. Armstrong—pretty bad hit, will be a cripple
3. Gonzales—who got it through the neck
4. Kromberg—in the leg
5. Richards—foot blown off
6. Fisken—who might die. Lost leg at the hip
7. Davies—who is paralyzed and will be crippled if he lives

And four more whose names I don't remember. Had funeral services at 1:00 P.M. but as I was on watch and couldn't go. Boy, our outfit is really catching hell. Also, Willheim, who went out of his mind. No wonder, as he came out of a hole where all the other fellows got killed. Moved into the tent, got set up, also we got a speaker for the radio. That's the way it goes, never know when you're going. Played cards after chow. Forty-five bombers (ours) flew over today. Twenty-four in one formation and 21 in the other. Also five transports landed on the field.

Monday, February 14, 1944

Well, Breski starts working with me in the morning. Davis came up and stayed all night. We got feeling good and Frank really got drunk. Had two air raids late last night and one early this morning. Heard those bombs coming down but they didn't land too close to us. Not raining either. Had an air raid later on in the evening but no harm done.

Tuesday, February 15, 1944

No air raids this morning. We had one around 10:20 A.M. this morning. Cleaned my rifle. Four LST came in with three cans. Got mail, one from the folks, Irene, Betty, and Glen. The planes only dropped a couple of eggs close enough to hear. Tucker cracked up and Gonzales lost his eye. Fisken and Davies are both going to live.

Wednesday, February 16, 1944

Had one air raid around 9:00 P.M. last night. Also got 100 razor blades from Jeanne. Played cards, pinochle as usual. Wrote a few letters and read for a little while. The way the bombers are going over every day, Tojo must be getting hell. Had an air raid at 11:25 A.M., awaiting developments now. That air raid we had hit an Aussie ship here and killed two men. Armstrong also left with Tucker.

Thursday, February 17, 1944

Got 900 replacements in yesterday and 10% of them were vets of Guadalcanal sent home and back out here again. Got fresh eggs, *butter,* and POTATOES and five smoked hams. Started making a ring today. Got mail, four letters from Reta, one from the folks, and one from Irene. In the afternoon I was feeling pretty sick. In the evening I was damn near frozen. I was shaking so much that they had to give me a shot of morphine.

Friday, February 18, 1944

Still sick and shaking this morning. They took me to the hospital and took a smear. It was positive, so I have malaria for the fourth time. They gave me eight atabrine and about six other pills. Walter's here and he taught me how to play acey-deucy. Also I met Gibson here. Boy, I sure do feel like hell and I ain't fooling. I got a toothbrush, powder, and blades here at the hospital.

Saturday, February 19, 1944

Well, this is my second day in the hospital. I'm feeling better than I was but still don't have much of an appetite. My one arm and hand have no strength; can hardly pick up anything and my fingers keep twitching. Wrote a letter to the folks.

The Accident 10

Sunday, February 20, 1944

Well, late last night I had a little bad luck. Going to the head, I fell in a bomb shelter. I can't walk on my foot; this afternoon they are going to x-ray it. Hope it isn't broken. Well, worse luck, it's broken. Doctor said it will be several weeks before I get out. Benton came to see me. La Valla came in today with malaria. What a life. Glad we're not in a liberty port.

Monday, February 21, 1944

Well, I did receive a little good news today. The doctor said they might put a cast on my foot and soon I could walk with the cast. But of course it will be some time before the cast can be taken off. Well, they gave me some crutches this afternoon and just before chow they gave me notice to go to surgery and they put a cast from my toe to my knee.

Tuesday, February 22, 1944

Well, Lutchie brought my mail over to me and later on Frank came to see me.

Wednesday, February 23, 1944

Well, Frank came down again today and brought me mail from Norm, folks, Irene, Reta, Ruth, and LaPore. That's about all. Wish like hell I could get out. They say part of our outfit has moved out and the rest might leave soon. If so, I'll see if my company can't get me out. If it's a blitz, I want to be in on it.

Thursday, February 24, 1944

Gee, I sure feel bad. They tell me that the 3rd Platoon of B Company is moving out. They will probably train in Oro Bay and maybe I'll be ready to meet them there before they shove off. I'd give anything to go on this next blitz, even a chance to go home!

Friday, February 25, 1944

Same old hospital routine. Some of the boys came down to see me. Pete sent down some coffee cake to me. Gee, it sure was good! Played poker in the afternoon. I won £2 and lent Lutchie £1. Wrote a few letters.

Saturday, February 26, 1944

Rained like hell all night long. Around 9:30 A.M. we had an air raid. Captain Fitzgerald came down to see us this morning. Wrote a couple of letters. Breski came down to see me. Brought me a pair of pants and cigarettes. Also Chaplain Fitzgerald came in to see me.

Sunday, February 27, 1944

Well, I have one consolation, today is my last day of treatment for malaria. They say the company is leaving March 4th for Cape Hoskins and I won't be able to go. I get all the breaks and they're all bad. Lutchie was evacuated today.

Monday, February 28, 1944

Well, I spent most of the day drawing some of Vargas girls and the rest of the time reading. We had *fresh ham* today, treats never cease, and fresh boiled potatoes. Breski came down in the afternoon to see me. He also brought me mail from Irene, Mrs. Peterson, Mrs. Panger, Nancy Lou, Jean (Australia), Reta (New Zealand), and Ruth Herre. Rained in the evening and throughout the night.

Tuesday, February 29, 1944

Well, it's raining again today which isn't surprising. I wrote a couple of letters, one to Irene and Nancy Lou. Later on in the afternoon I did a little drawing. Saw LaGasse down here, he strained his back and that just about winds up a wet day. Still no air raids. What's the matter, Tojo?

Wednesday, March 1, 1944

Well, the company is supposed to shove off today. Boy, I begged the doctor to let me out but he couldn't see it. It sure is hell staying behind when you know your outfit is shoving off and probably into action. What I wouldn't give to be going with them. Still raining.

Thursday, March 2, 1944

It's still raining. I guess that's about all it has in the Godforsaken hole. It sure is surprising the number of boys that they have in the hospital here. And their spirit and the way they take their injuries are certainly remarkable. Drew a couple of Vargas girls today.

Friday, March 3, 1944

Raining still. Heard the 2nd Battalion 7th is going up to the Admiralty Islands to help the Doggies out as they're in trouble as usual and have to call on the Marines to fight their battles for them. Hope I get a chance to go up there or Cape Hoskins. The boys are way past Borgen Bay, they're all the way down to Talasea.

Saturday, March 4, 1944

Well, I went back to camp today. It sure looks deserted with ¾ of the company gone and tents down, etc. Got Walter's acey-deucy game off him. Also got some stationery off of the boys. Mail came in but I didn't receive any. In the evening Jack, Smokey, and I played cards and listened to the radio. Rained all day long.

Sunday, March 5, 1944

Well, they took my cast off this morning. Have to use crutches now. Wish he would put on another cast or do something. Jack, Smokey, and I played cards all afternoon. In the evening we played cards and listened to the radio. Rained all day.

Monday, March 6, 1944

Well, they sent Jack down to the 30th Evacuation Hospital today as they are shipping him out. My ankle is sure hurting like hell, he better do something about it. Well, Jack came back as just stretcher cases are going out by air. He will stay here until the ships come in. Night we played cards and listened to the radio. Rained.

Tuesday, March 7, 1944

Well, he put a cast on this morning and he fouled it up so he had to cut it off and put another one on in the afternoon. Saw a lot of Aussie planes come in today. So far, 14 Jap planes have been shot down at night here. Two guns have five planes apiece and the other one has four and one probably.

Wednesday, March 8, 1944

Well, I guess good old B Company is in action down at Talasea. They are just 160 miles from Rabaul and also the Doggies made 43 miles of advancement from Arawe. The Japs must have evacuated. They brought back 20 more casualties from Talasea. They ran into two Jap regiments. Played cards in the evening.

Thursday, March 9, 1944

Well, the 3rd Battalion 1st Marines and one Company from the 7th Marines are going on a blitz. I went to camp today and brought back some cake, also I had a good piece of fresh steak. Jack left at 6:30 A.M. to go to Brisbane by plane. He came back in the afternoon as the plane didn't come in. Scronski got evacuated to the States. Trick knee; they are going to put a celluloid plate over his knee cap. Rained again.

Friday, March 10, 1944

Well, for a change it didn't rain again today, but was nice all day long. Met a fellow sergeant from the NCO mess in Balcombe; he's in Signal Company. Wish I would get some mail soon. Just lay around all day and read as I was lucky enough to get hold of some reading material.

Saturday, March 11, 1944

Well, it happened for a change, it didn't rain. Lay around all day as I have to stay off my foot as much as possible. Get quite a kick out of listening to Madam Tojo. She calls us "Bloody Butchers of Guadalcanal" and "Orphans of the Southwest Pacific." I awoke in the middle of the night to find a big rat on my foot. I got rid of him in a hurry. This place is lousy with them.

Sunday, March 12, 1944

Company C 1st Battalion 7th Marines down near Hill 660 had 39 men left out of a Company of around 190. They sure took a beating. I know two of them that got killed really well. It sure is a beautiful day today. P. P. Davis brought me some mail today. Two from Eileen, one from Jeanne, and three from the folks. Lost quite a few boys from typhoid, only know of one that got it and lived. Battle of Death Valley.

Monday, March 13, 1944

Well, nothing much happened during the day; it didn't rain for a change. Just lay around all day. Played acey-deucy. Around 4:00 P.M. we had an air raid which didn't last long. So far we have 340 Marines planted in our cemetery.

Tuesday, March 14, 1944

Well, Davis came down to see me today. He brought me some candy, carton of cigarettes, matches, and some reading material. No mail. I guess we've got it but nobody sending it up from Oro Bay, New Guinea. Played acey-deucy all afternoon. Heard B Company is supposed to come back this week.

Wednesday, March 15, 1944

Well, it rained today off and on all day long. Read most of the day. Wrote a couple of letters. Evacuated five more fellows from my ward. Saw Kromberg in here, he was wounded down at C Company. Doctor said I would be in here for a while yet.

Thursday, March 16, 1944

Well, it rained again today as per usual. We had an air raid around 9:00 P.M. Down at Talasea, Ski got shot in the hand and Meloklech cracked up. They say the Aussies are coming in as they want to take Rabaul. Smokey is going down to the 30th evacuation. That's about all for today. Wrote a letter to the folks.

Friday, March 17, 1944

Wrote a letter to the folks and wrote one to Irene and Peggy. In the afternoon we played acey-deucy all day long. In the evening we played cards and listened to the radio.

Saturday, March 18, 1944

Well, first off I went to camp this morning. I finally got some mail, two from the folks, three from Irene, one from Reta (New Zealand), and one from Betty (Australia). Had an air raid. He dropped five eggs. There were two of them; one was shot down by one of our P40 Warhawks. Also received my citation from Guadalcanal.

Sunday, March 19, 1944

Wrote a letter to Irene, Reta, and folks, also my good friend Brad left the hospital this morning. Address: P.F.C. Edward Bratsch—Weapons Company 7th Marines. That's about all for now. Lay around all day, read! A nice day, no rain and no air raid. I could stand the air raid though as it's deader than hell around here. So concludes another day in the war zone.

Monday, March 20, 1944

Just about the same old routine. It rained again today. I went to church here last night. We sure have a nice chaplain. Went to camp today and got a few letters, the greatest morale builder there is. Also received a Christmas package from some people in California.

Tuesday, March 21, 1944

They were going to take my cast off today but they x-rayed it and it's still fractured. Also I got all of my pictures fixed up today and I sure have got some honeys. They say we'll only be here from six weeks to three months now.

Wednesday, March 22, 1944

Well, I got two letters today, one from the folks and one from Sydney and a few toilet articles. Also took one of the gooks out and took his picture. Having them fixed up after chow. Wrote a couple of letters and played acey-deucy.

Thursday, March 23, 1944

Well, the day passed quite uneventful. It rained most of the forenoon. In the morning I got some shots of the gooks and got them fixed up, they sure came out good. In the evening I read *The Case of the Velvet Claws,* by Erle Stanley Gardner; it's another Perry Mason novel.

Friday, March 24, 1944

Well, I took my cast off yesterday. In the afternoon, Bivins brought me some mail down. Two from the folks and one from Irene. The Bulldozer killed a small python yesterday. It rained all night long and most of the day, clearing up in the late afternoon.

Saturday, March 25, 1944

Well, it rained again on and off all day long. They took me over to surgery and took another x-ray of my ankle but didn't say what the outcome of it was. I wrote a couple of letters in the afternoon and I read a book called *Enter a Murderer,* by Ngaio Marsh.

Sunday, March 26, 1944

Well, same sort of day, it rained again to make it complete. I went to church in the evening but we didn't have any service as the chaplain couldn't make it. Although it makes a pretty scene, a lot of men sitting on the ground with a rough altar of branches and palm fronds with palm trees and jungles behind it and the sun setting and the mountains in the distant background.

Monday, March 27, 1944

Well, old Murphy is leaving tomorrow for Brisbane via States. One thing, it's interesting to talk to different fellows, some of the things they do and have done really takes the cake. Some of the fellows in the 11th killed two big snakes, one six feet long and the other nearly five feet. There sure are a lot of them around here. Scuttlebutt is that we're going on another blitz. I sure hope it's the Caroline Islands or New Ireland.

Tuesday, March 28, 1944

I have my gook friend doing my laundry for me. His name is Sul-Me and he's quite a character. He does my laundry for a shilling which is equivalent to about 16 cents. Two suits of clothes, one suit of underwear and a pair of socks. Also I wrote a letter to Irene. Well, it really is a beautiful day today. The doctor said my ankle was a nasty break, that is, the break in my ankle.

Wednesday, March 29, 1944

Raining again today, practically continuous, which never raised the morale of the troops. Last night a fellow in our ward got epileptic fits. I wrote a letter to the folks, Irene, Jeanne, and Frances. My hair is starting to come in fairly good now. I sure massage it good every night and it seems to be coming in a little thicker. A little mail came in; I don't know if I received any or not.

Thursday, March 30, 1944

We're not allowed to say, "I was in on the initial invasion of Cape Gloucester." Well, the doctor said today nothing he could do, I would just have to rest as it takes time to heal. Passed the day reading and writing letters. We haven't had any mail for quite some time now.

Friday, March 31, 1944

Well, I sure felt bad all day long. I think I had a slight attack of malaria but I'm not going to say anything about it. Over the radio today we heard the Army hit an atoll in the Carolina Islands group. Hope we go on another blitz from here.

Saturday, April 1, 1944

Well, here's the fourth month of this year already. Boy, times sure goes by quick. Well, we finally got some mail in today. I received two from the folks, one from Irene, and one from Tebbe, and also a registered letter from Peggy with some snapshots I took when I was there. I drew a sketch of the head, my scenic view from my sack.

Sunday, April 2, 1944

Well, it's Sunday and it just seems to be in the air that it is. It's a beautiful warm day and everything seems so quiet and peaceful, that it's hard to imagine that a few months ago this was the scene of a bloody battleground with men fighting and dying, sweating, cursing, and killing. Most of the boys seem content to just lie around as there is no work or drill today. Not worrying about the future or what it has in store for them. Funny how you can look back at the fellows killed and the sight of the cemetery with all those white crosses and not feel very deeply. I guess because you get used to seeing men dead, dying, and mutilated. Corpse rotting and decaying, covered with big flies and maggots; something that the people at home will never experience.

Monday, April 3, 1944

Well, I went to church yesterday again as it was Palm Sunday. Services were held earlier than usual. At 4:30 P.M. just as services were closing, a Zero sneaked in and dropped an egg. One of the doctors died day before yesterday. He was shot in the stomach at Talasea. Another white cross added to the vast number there now. Rained last night and this morning.

Tuesday, April 4, 1944

Well, got a letter from Frances today. I wrote a couple and started making a P-38. Also I got a pair of boondockers as I only had one good shoe left. Rained all night and a good part of the day. I walked a little on my foot. It was like a stick in the breeze and weak as hell. I nearly fell a couple of times.

Wednesday, April 5, 1944

Well, it really rained all day long. Got some mail in. Three from the folks, one from Mrs. Panger, Tebbe, and *The Home Town Bugle.* And the treat we had today was *ICE CREAM!* The first we have had since last October. Finished my P-38 and it really looks pretty good. From now on they say patients are going to get ice cream every day.

Thursday, April 6, 1944

The day started out swell. I started making a matchbox holder. Wrote a few letters. The chow is really lousy. Coffee, no milk for it and you get sugar if you're lucky. Fish, corned beef, beans, potatoes. Sure will be glad when I can get a good meal every day.

Friday, April 7, 1944

Well, it rained again today as is the usual procedure of rain daily. Nothing was accomplished today except that I managed to dash off a few letters. My period of rest is rapidly drawing to an end. Washed a few clothes and in the evening I heard the radio which I thoroughly enjoyed.

Saturday, April 8, 1944

Well, it really started out nice this morning. It reminded one of home in the fall. Leaves are changing color and falling and you can hear the locusts throughout the day shattered by the occasional roar of a plane overhead going into a dive or performing some sort of stunt flying.

Sunday, April 9, 1944

Well, today is Easter Sunday and they didn't have church services down here so I missed them. In the next tent one fellow had a banjo and the other a violin and they really gave out for us. A centipede five inches long was on me today and did I jump! They're not poisonous but will make you deathly sick if they sting you. We had ice cream and fresh potatoes and meat for supper.

Monday, April 10, 1944

Well, it started out nice today with fresh eggs for breakfast and the sun shining. Around noon the day grew dismal with rain. Fish and carrots for dinner. If I never see fish or corned beef again, it will be too soon. Got mail, one from Irene and one from Eileen. Had some ice cream again. Madam Tojo's Zero Hour is right on. She says, "For men in the Southwest Pacific who have wandered too far from home."

Tuesday, April 11, 1944

A lot of scuttlebutt is flying around that we're leaving here the end of this month. Destination so say, Russell Island, Guadalcanal, Marshall Islands, Pearl Harbor, Australia, States; take your pick. Also a lot of talk about invasion of the Philippine Islands. Have a native here slashed up pretty bad; he was attacked by a wild boar. Snakes are quite plentiful in the surrounding jungle and often found in camps. The Marine Orchestra played for us yesterday afternoon. American Patrol outside of town.

Wednesday, April 12, 1944

Saw my first show in over 4 ½ months, *Corvette K-225,* which I thoroughly enjoyed. Also got mail, four from Irene, four folks, from Jeanne, Reta, and one from Nancy Lou, also I had another x-ray taken of my ankle. Also a package from Eileen. Guess we are going to Guadalcanal as some of our officers are leaving in the morning. We're supposed to have 135 new Amphs there, 35 with 37 MM on them.

Thursday, April 13, 1944

Well, two more of the boys from my outfit are down here in the hospital with me now. Rained again as per usual. Played cards in the afternoon. Read a book, *The Blonde Died First.* And so another day ends. Heard that the division received another citation, also my battalion. New Britain: 442 killed, 10 missing, and 1,052 wounded.

Friday, April 14, 1944

Also heard 10,000 Japs were killed, an average of 20 to 1. Received a couple of letters, one from Reta, and one from Nancy Lou. Rained again today. Played cards and read. Guess I'll get out next week. Also read *The Case of the Substitute Face,* by Erle Stanley Gardner.

Saturday, April 15, 1944

Well nothing happened much today. Guess I'll be out in a couple of days now. We're to leave here and go to Guadalcanal in a week to 10 days.

Sunday, April 16, 1944

I went to camp today and saw some of the boys and received two letters, one from Irene and one from Nancy Lou. I sure feel like hell, tossed my cookies and have a hell of a chill. I think the old bug has got me again.

Monday, April 17, 1944

Don't believe I ever felt so bad in my life, not only malaria but dysentery with it. Either at head or else tossing my cookies. Feel like I'm going to die and wish I could. Got two V-mails from the folks.

Tuesday, April 18, 1944

Sure am sick, tried to write some letters but I am too shaky. Still can't keep anything down.

Wednesday, April 19, 1944

Well, at breakfast I ate a little and managed to keep a little down and by supper time I had been able to eat nearly half of my supper. Read *Trial by Fury,* by Craig Rice.

Thursday, April 20, 1944

Well, I'm just about back to my old self now. The doctor is trying to get me evacuated on account of malaria. But they're not going to evacuate any more men until we reach our new destination. Wrote a few letters today.

Friday, April 21, 1944

Last night I went to the show and saw *Winterland,* and also a newsreel of our landing here. Went to camp today and got a haircut. Came back and wrote a few letters. The rest of the afternoon I spent reading.

Saturday, April 22, 1944

Well, nothing out of the ordinary today. The outfit is going to shove off tomorrow so I guess I'll get out of the hospital.

Sunday, April 23, 1944

Well, I got released from the hospital today, with a four-day no-duty slip. Got back to camp, all my souvenirs were gone and most of my clothes, rifle, equipment, mess gear, and blanket. We're really leaving and I'm anxious to get on the ship once more. Will be working all day long. Leave in the morning. Supper is our last meal.

Chapter 4

Destination Pavuvu 11

Monday, April 24, 1944

Well, we broke camp around 8:00 A.M. and went down to the beach. Went out to the ship around 12:00 P.M. and had to come back in as they wouldn't allow us aboard. No sleep sitting on top of supplies and it rained all night long. Had rations for breakfast. 40th Army is relieving us. They have 22 months overseas and haven't seen any action as yet. How about that?

Tuesday, April 25, 1944

Well, we're aboard the *President Jackson*. Fairly good chow, no work, ice cold water. Sleeping compartment is a sweat box. Saw a movie, *The St. Returns.* Going to the PX today. At 1:00 A.M. we're supposed to drag anchor and shove off.

Wednesday, April 26, 1944

Rained like hell all day long. Supposed to dock tomorrow. Saw *Torrid Zone* night before last and *Dressed to Kill* last night. Bought ice cream and candy and cigars and peanuts. It's still raining quite hard and a little rough. Wish it would get rougher than hell.

Thursday, April 27, 1944

Well, this is our last day aboard ship, positively. We drew rations for one day, which means we get off the ship tomorrow morning. I suppose it's another tropical sweat box. But that's life for you in the tropics. Oh, Hell!!!

Friday, April 28, 1944

Well, we had reveille at 3:30 A.M. this morning and ate chow at 4:00 A.M. At 8:00 A.M. we got off the ship at the Russell Islands and got to shore at about 9:20 A.M. and then we headed for our new area. Kind of a nice island, it's a lot like New Hebrides and plenty of flies.

Saturday, April 29, 1944

My ankle is bothering me like hell so I turned into sick bay and got a no-duty slip. Paul is going to give me some turtle rings from Talasea.

Sunday, April 30, 1944

Well, Collins tried to get me run up because I had no duty and went to the show. So the doctor said I was on full duty until an x-ray could be taken of my foot. If I ever catch him alone, I'm going to give him the beating of his life.

Monday, May 1, 1944

Well, I went to work at noon today. My ankle is hurting me like hell but I'll be darned if I'll say anything. I received mail today, four from Irene, four from the folks, and one from the people on the West Coast. Breski left today for the hospital. He's going Stateside.

Tuesday, May 2, 1944

Read *Behind That Curtain,* by Earl Derr Biggers. It's a Charlie Chan mystery. Wrote to Irene and the people on the West Coast, also will try to write to the folks. Went to work at noon. What a hole, raining all the time, our tent leaks from shrapnel holes and mud up to the top of your shoes and flies galore.

Wednesday, May 3, 1944

Well, I took some pictures and negatives that I took. One roll out of three was good, the rest were wet. Spent most of the morning down by the ocean just resting and enjoying Mother Nature. Picked up a few odd shells. Seven liberty ships came in with some more of the 1st Marine Division.

Thursday, May 4, 1944

Well, it rained again today. This sure is a mud hole. It's up to your ankles and in some places a lot deeper. The boys killed a young calf. It was bogged down in the mud. We butchered it and barbecued it and was it good. Saw Ted Lewis in *Is Everybody Happy?*

Friday, May 5, 1944

The name of this island is Pavuvu (*P A V U V U*), one of the Russell Islands. Breski came up to see us. He's still in the hospital. The general flew in today. All it does here is rain and then rain some more. In the evening we went to the show and saw Hopalong Cassidy in *Lost Canyon.*

Saturday, May 6, 1944

Pavuvu—means "Pearl of the Pacific." Was British prior to being one of the Russell Island group. Ships are coming in tomorrow, a little mail came in. I got a V-mail from the folks. The rain is still coming. It just won't stop. Pigs are the only thing that could live in the mud and enjoy it.

Sunday, May 7, 1944

Well, the rain is still with us, also the mud. My ankle is still bothering me. Worked from 3:30 A.M. till one and then we had to put up our tent and dig a trench around it so our sacks wouldn't float away. In the evening, went to the show but it was called off as ships came in and they needed the men to unload ships.

Monday, May 8, 1944

Well, mail came in. I received two letters from Irene and one from Joan. I also answered them right away. Raining again. Had to wash my shoes, socks, and pants as I went in muck up to my knees. God, I hate this place. It isn't fit for man or beast. Had a small earthquake yesterday, I thought the ground was going to fall in.

Tuesday, May 9, 1944

Well, it rained practically all day again today. Nothing unusual happened today. Mail came in again and of course I got some mail. Airmail letter to Australia now costs 70 cents, regular 5 cents. Went to the show in the evening and saw one of the best pictures I ever saw, *Flying High,* with Dick Powell and Dorothy Lamour.

Wednesday, May 10, 1944

Well, fresh meat came in plus fresh butter. Eighteen hundred pounds of meat. Had pork chops for supper with steak (beef). Had one beef tenderloin steak and five pork chops and two loin lamb chops. Roast lamb, mashed potatoes, gravy, coffee, toast, and butter for breakfast. Hamburgers for dinner and roast beef for supper. Rained again. Had a snake in my tent above my sack last night.

Thursday, May 11, 1944

Well, I got a letter from Tebbe and one from Jeanne and one from Amy. A Liberator dropped quite a few bombs today. We could feel the ground tremble here. Also, picture of Betty which was sure beat up.

Friday, May 12, 1944

Well, we can now say every place we've been to, but just one in each letter. I sent home some "Jap money," memoirs of Melbourne, New Zealand postcards, and snaps of Peg and me. It just sprinkled very lightly. Wrote about six letters. In the evening I went to the show and saw *No Time for Love,* Fred MacMurray and Claudette Colbert, which was right on the ball.

Saturday, May 13, 1944

Didn't work much today. Grilled hotcakes from 5:00 until 9:00 A.M. Started at 3:30 A.M. Ate breakfast and go to work tomorrow afternoon; pretty soft for a change. Got mail from Tebbe, folks and Irene. Wrote to all of them. Going to the show tonight. Saw Joe E. Brown in *Casanova of the Burlesque,* which was a really good show. Rained but just a little.

Sunday, May 14, 1944

Well, today was a very nice day, in the evening it was really wonderful as we got our ration of beer and Pepsi Cola. Eight beers and four Pepsis and I traded some for beer making 12 and got three more making 15 bottles of beer. I got feeling pretty good, in fact, it was wonderful.

Monday, May 15, 1944

Well, I sent home my bayonet today plus five registered letters, also I started sending home some of my negatives. Sent eight today and am sending home 16 tomorrow. Earl Rowe came up and I had a few beers left that we finished. In the evening I went to see him as they drew theirs. I had six bottles. Then went to the show and saw *On Parade,* with Kay Kyser.

Tuesday, May 16, 1944

Earle gave two pairs of pants and two shirts, bottle of cordial and two cartons of Philip Morris and a carton of matches. Put up my hammock. Nelson is fixing up my P-38 for me. No rain yesterday or today so far. Went to the show and saw *Moonlight in Vermont.*

Wednesday, May 17, 1944

Well, I drew $435.00 and I finally collected the $29.00 Mock owed me as he owed it to me for about one year and four months. Sent home some more pictures. In the evening we went to the show and saw *Girl of the Golden West.* Came back and played pinochle for a dollar a game, I came out $1.00 ahead.

Thursday, May 18, 1944

Sent home one more letter. Had the afternoon off and went down to see Commander Peabody, world's greatest banjo player. Came back and the galley was on fire as a stove exploded. What a sight. Smoke could be seen a couple of blocks away. Went to the show in the evening and saw *Song of Bernadette,* which was really a wonderful picture.

Friday, May 19, 1944

Well, first off at about 5:30 A.M., I got both of my legs scalded. In the afternoon I made out a money order for $400.00. Got a letter from Reta. Washed clothes and played cards for money of course. Played cards again in the evening and won 50 cents. Also it rained all night.

Saturday, May 20, 1944

Just another day that passed. I sent home that $400.00 and some more pictures. Worked as usual and wrote a few letters. In the evening we played cards again as per usual and I lost 50 cents so that makes us even.

Sunday, May 21, 1944

Well, here it is Sunday again. I wanted to get baptized today but I couldn't get off. Maybe I can make it next Sunday. Worked until noon. Slept a little. Took a shower and washed clothes. Got both of my legs scalded. Woe is me. Played cards in the evening, ended up even. Major Cooper left us to be stationed in Washington, D.C.

Monday, May 22, 1944

Well, mail came in today but I didn't get any. In the evening I went to the show to see *Submarine Base,* but it rained and I got drenched. I walked two miles to see it and got wet—but definitely. Was like a young cyclone, the wind nearly blew you over. Rain was coming down so hard you couldn't see more than 20 feet in front of you.

Tuesday, May 23, 1944

Moved to another tent today. I really built a swell table so we could write on it. Lost the stone out of Tom's watch ring. Sure felt bad about it. Got one letter from Irene today. Went to the show in the evening, *Beautiful but Broke,* and it really was good, with Joan Davis and three other clowns.

Wednesday, May 24, 1944

Boy, this cold is really getting me down. Have three officers going home. Lieutenant Peterson, H. Sawyer, and Lieutenant Ames. I'd sure like to be going home. In the evening I saw the picture *Hey, Rookie,* which was really good. Well, we just got word Val is going home now, he's to leave at 6:15 A.M. tomorrow; he's going out by plane. Boy, is he happy and excited. Good!!!!

Thursday, May 25, 1944

Well, Valincourt left this morning and was he happy! I guess you know I would be too. Went to the PX, I didn't get much but I did get a mirror and comb. In the evening we went to the show and saw *Tarzan's Desert Mystery.* Also a stage show put on by some of the Army boys who came over from Guadalcanal. One clown there was from Barnum and Bailey. Also "Tribal Strange," who really could sing.

Friday, May 26, 1944

Well, here we are starting another day. Wrote a few letters. I'm going over to the PX after awhile. Got fresh meat. Cattle that they killed here on the island. The water is terrible, we set cans out and catch rain water. Do we purify it? Don't be a silly a____. Wrote a letter to Marguerite in the evening and read a book. Went to the PX, got towel, candy, shoestrings, shave lotion, and peanuts. Cost $4.50.

Saturday, May 27, 1944

Well, here we go again, not much left of this month. Well, Price and Rocases went over to Banika, said they had a good time and also ran into a couple of Army nurses. In the evening I went to the show and saw *See Here, Private Hargrove,* which was a good show and I enjoyed it very much.

Sunday, May 28, 1944

Well, it certainly is a beautiful day today. Received a V-mail from Johnny Blechart's sister-in-law with his address and a letter from Tebbe. Wrote a few letters myself.

Monday, May 29, 1944

Well nothing much happened today. They are going to open the officer's mess tomorrow. Also I am going to go over to Banika, it takes 1 ¾ hours one way by boat. Going on the mail boat. Leaving camp at 6:00 A.M. and leaving the dock at 6:45 A.M.

Tuesday, May 30, 1944

Well, up bright and early this morning. Left the docks at 6:45 A.M. and go to Banika at 8:30 A.M. Went 12 miles inland to the airport which is very large and sure is swell. Tried to get in a bomber and go on a mission, but no soap. Saw our new Buffaloes with a turret in them, a 37 MM gun and one air cooled .30 caliber alongside it. Two .50 caliber in the back of it. Went to the Red Cross and saw three white women, one blond, sure was nice looking. Had to go through a channel, saw two sharks and some pretty blue starfish. Blue minnows and some pretty tropical fish. In the evening, went to the show and saw *Meet the People,* with Dick Powell, Lucille Ball, and Virginia Bruce.

Wednesday, May 31, 1944

Nothing much doing, got two V-mails from home. Rained all day long. Sure am tired out. Shot in the afternoon. Went to the show in the evening and saw *Chip off the Old Block.*

Thursday, June 1, 1944

Got two letters from Irene and answered one of them. Quite a few of the old boys going home tomorrow. Lucky!!! What!!! Oh, well, more power to them. In the evening, I was pretty tired so I stayed in, played cards for £50 a game and came out even. Made me a gadget which I think I can catch a starfish in. I hope!

Friday, June 2, 1944

Well, the Chief and two Corpsmen left and also Victor Savior the Baker. So that's four more less of the old boys. That makes 11 old boys gone home from here. Got a letter from Beryll, one from Betty, and two from the folks. Wrote some letters in the afternoon.

Saturday, June 3, 1944

Well, we got fresh meat in today. And of course, I had to cut it up and my hand is infected and sore as hell and it didn't do it any good. I went on the native run to try and get some star fish but it was too deep. Saw five sharks and quite a few barracuda and I wasn't going to dive for them with those guys hanging around.

Sunday, June 4, 1944

Well, worked till noon today; had a turkey pot pie. Canned turkey of course but it sure was good. My hand is so sore, I can hardly write. My finger is nearly three times its normal size. Got mail, Tebbe, Irene, and Reta. Going to the show tonight. Saw *Larceny with Music,* and *A Guy Named Joe,* which was really a wonderful picture.

Monday, June 5, 1944

Well, fresh meat today, steak for dinner and hamburgers for supper. Got my drawing stuff from home today. My hand is stilled fouled up. Meat came in again. Have to cut meat after dark tomorrow.

Tuesday, June 6, 1944

Well, today I sent home two packages. One a bayonet and the other a raincoat, canteen, belt, and an armory container. Worked until noon. Got a letter from Tebbe. Went to the show in the evening, saw *Best Foot Forward,* which was right on. Drew a picture today. The allies hit in France, made 15 beachheads along a 200 mile front.

Wednesday, June 7, 1944

Day passed as usual. We got 12 replacements in today. We're going to add one more company to our battalion, the company will be known as "Dog Company," which they say is going to consist of "Doggies." How about that?

Thursday, June 8, 1944

Well, it rained today. Davis heard from Val, he's aboard ship via States. Heard from Tebbe and received a couple of patches from him. Rained like hell most all day. Played cards, lost only $1.25 so that's not bad. Sent home two packages.

Friday, June 9, 1944

Well, June is moving right along. Rained again today, this sure is a mud hole. Rieser and Jones are both getting out of the galley. Today is Rieser's last day. Went to the show in the evening and saw Bing Crosby in *Come Along with Me,* and also *Friendly Enemies.* Received a package from home.

Saturday, June 10, 1944

No rain today. Big inspection by major. Lot of scuttlebutt going around about going home, but I don't think so. They told me I'm going to get the next rate that comes out or in other words, staff sergeant. Don't know though. No show tonight so I stayed in camp and fiddled around. Bought two coconuts for $2.00 apiece.

Sunday, June 11, 1944

Well, it rained quite a bit today. Jones got out of the galley today. Got mail. Received snapshots of Irene and Val. Sent home my watch, coins, and Tom's ring. In the evening, I went to the show and saw *Lure of the Islands* and *Standing Room Only.* Also we got in some Navy men and flame throwers.

Monday, June 12, 1944

Worked till noon and then I wrote some letters and read for awhile. Washed clothes and took a shower. In the evening, I went to the 8th Marines to see a stage show.

Tuesday, June 13, 1944

Well, we got 40 Doggies in today. They are going to A Company with us operating ducks with rockets. In the evening we went to the movies and saw *Cover Girl;* had to leave before it was over as 86 Doggies came in around 9:00 P.M. and we had to get chow for them. If it had been us, we'd have gone hungry as we have more than once already.

Wednesday, June 14, 1944

Had to get up at 2:00 A.M., worked like hell all day until noon, then I sacked in for the day. In the evening we saw *Nine Girls,* a pretty good show.

Thursday, June 15, 1944

Well, today went along as good as could be expected. It rained quite a bit today. More coming in soon. Sent Mother $20.00 for the pictures. Received two letters from Irene today. In the evening, I wrote a letter to Irene and one to the folks. Went to bed early.

Friday, June 16, 1944

Well, nothing unusual happened today. I sent home $20.00 to take care of those pictures. *Hi, Good Lookin'!* was the show I saw in the evening which was pretty good.

Saturday, June 17, 1944

Well, 35 more Doggies came in today, also I bought some pictures of some natives and in the evening I went and saw *Cover Girl,* as last time I had to leave in the middle of the show to feed those Doggies. Got in three new Buffaloes with a ramp in the rear. Also they bombed Japan and Marines landed in the Mariana Islands.

Sunday, June 18, 1944

Well, it's really a beautiful day today. No mail came in. Got two more coolers from the Aussies. Rained a little in the afternoon. In the evening I saw *Night Raid in Arabia.*

Monday, June 19, 1944

Well, today it rained quite a bit. I sent home those 12 native pictures I bought off a native. Got two letters from Irene. Stayed home in the evening.

Tuesday, June 20, 1944

Well, I finally go a roll of film developed by a Doggie. Played horseshoes, in the evening, went to the show and saw *Lady in the Dark.*

Wednesday, June 21, 1944

Well, today it rained in the morning. I went to the PX. Got mail from Johnny, Norm, Reta, and hometown paper. Played horseshoes and worked, of course. Have an appointment with the dentist tomorrow. In the evening saw *Two Girls and a Sailor,* with Virginia O'Brien. What a woman.

Thursday, June 22, 1944

Well, nothing much happened today. Victor Savior came back as they're not sending any more home that are serving here. Washed clothes again. As usual in the evening I went to see *Gung Ho,* as we were aboard ship with them when we left Guadalcanal.

Friday, June 23, 1944

Well, another day. Talk about rain, it rained like hell today. Won't go home this time, that's certain. Saw the picture *Lady, Let's Dance.* Got a letter from Margaret Ann and Frances. So another day dissolves. Some more boys going home tomorrow, not from our outfit.

Saturday, June 24, 1944

Had chicken today and what a job I had cleaning them and after they were cooked, cutting them up. No mail today. Supposed to go to school on driving the Buffalo but it was called off. In the evening I saw Olivia de Havilland in *Princess O'Rourke,* which was a swell picture.

Sent home:
January 10th clipping and stamp
January 11th Cartoon, Christmas card, matchbox, and postcard.
January 11th postcards and picture of Jap soldier
January 19th Jap woman and double postcard of Jap landing
January 20th box—Jap celluloid container with cat's-eyes, 20 or so postcards, 3 Jap ditty bags, plus big scarf. Two 2nd class private emblems, shells, towels, toothbrushes, 2 ice containers
January 30th 5 Jap snapshots, also package with, Jap shirt, socks, bayonet, scabbard, shells. 3rd package with native board
May 12th 4 Jap bills, American $2.00 bill.
May 13th 5 snapshots of Regiment, my Thanks for the Memories snapshots of New Zealand.
May 14th Peg & Jean, 4 clippings of Marines in Australia, 4 regular letters
May 15th sent home Jap bayonet
May 16th New Guinea gold
May 17th negatives, and New Caledonia money

Sunday, June 25, 1944

Sure is a beautiful day today. Our new mess hall and galley is sure coming along. It's being built by the Navy Seabee's. It's all going to be screened in. The Army has their new duck coming in. I mean they arrived today, 50 of them. We're supposed to get a couple of hundred new Buffaloes in. Next blitz is going to be something. Latest dope is around the end of August or first part of September. Saw *Bridge of San Luis Rey.*

Monday, June 26, 1944

Well, today I signed for a package. Took a roll of snaps. Sure was a hell of a hot day. Got a letter from Mona today. Chow is getting low, no bread—hardtack, no coffee. Hope we draw some tomorrow. Was down on the beach all afternoon. Drew equipment today—canteens, poncho, helmet, pack, first aid pack. We're standing by as reinforcements. I guess for Saipan as that's about the only place they're fighting. I sure hope that we go but soon. Saw *The Devil with Hitler* and another short.

Tuesday, June 27, 1944

Well, it was just another day, we had our usual rain. I received a package from home with a knife from Dad. Drew some more equipment, bayonet, canteens, first aid pack. They demonstrated with our flame throwers today. God, I'd hate to be in front of one of them. We have three, one for each company. Saw a show in the evening, *Battle of China.*

Wednesday, June 28, 1944

Well, we got word from the Corps that we're to send home 12 men per month so as its two months old we're about ready to send home 36 men. Drew a pad today, it sure is comfortable. Got a letter from the folks. Went to the show and saw *Four Jills in a Jeep,* which was a good picture.

Thursday, June 29, 1944

Well, today I watched them fire the flame throwers once more. Boy, it sure is on the ball. Hate like hell to be on the receiving end of them. In the evening, I went down to the docks and saw Allan Jones in *Rhythm of the Islands.* Rained as usual.

Friday, June 30, 1944

Well, this winds up another month. Worked until noon and then I went down to the beach, only found two shells though. In the evening I saw Mickey Rooney in *Blonde Trouble,* was good but it rained like hell and then the picture broke down a few times.

Saturday, July 1, 1944

Well, inspection today and also they gave out Purple Hearts for the boys who were wounded on the last blitz. Got hold of five beautiful cat's-eyes, they really are nice. Pictures didn't come out at all! Went to the show in the evening and saw a swell picture and stage show, *The Great Impersonation.*

Sunday, July 2, 1944

Another Sunday and another beautiful day. Worked until noon. Hear we're going to get another Army Company and one Amphibian Cargo Carrier and one Amphibian Armored Unit with turrets and 37 MM. Sounds like this next blitz is going to be something to see and I don't mean maybe. Marines had heaviest losses in the Corps history at Saipan.

Monday, July 3, 1944

Well, today I received two letters from Marguerite and also a very nice picture. Wrote a few letters. Supposed to get beer in today but now they say we're going to get it tomorrow. Have another Army Duck outfit coming in, the 454th. 26 men came in today. The one we have here is the 457th. Didn't go to the show, stayed in camp and wrote letters.

Tuesday, July 4, 1944

Boys' morale is really low. I mean the old boys. They went to see the chaplain to see why we're the only ones not being relieved. In the evening, I went down to the docks and saw seven boxing matches. Then we had the 1st Division Band and after that a picture show. Got back to camp around 10:45 P.M.

Wednesday, July 5, 1944

Well, a fellow in the 7th Marines shot his captain with a tommy gun. Kid was going home, then the captain told him he took his name off and the kid killed him. Had an air raid, I think it was just a drill, anyway, nothing happened. Went to the show in the evening and saw Frank Sinatra in *Higher and Higher,* which I didn't care for very much.

Thursday, July 6, 1944

Well, from now on we have no more chief cooks. Next rate is Mess Staff Sergeant. Teddy, Walter, Miller, Breski, Davis, Myhan, Erlick, Peterson, and 15 other men are going home tomorrow at 6:00 A.M. I bought Myhan's watch, an Elgin which I paid $40.00 for, also got his locker, box, pillow, pen, and stationery. They are going to send 150 more men home before the next big push.

Friday, July 7, 1944

Well, the boys left early this morning and were they happy. Sent home $100.00. I'm now running one watch and a Doggie the other. Fed 809 men all total. Had to move to another tent this morning. Bought a box of cigars and sold them for $1.00 profit. Sent home my coconut. Wrote a few letters. Sent out my laundry. Went to the show and saw *Jam Session.*

Saturday, July 8, 1944

Well, another day another dollar. Sure had a tough day today. Got mail from Irene, folks, Tebbe, Mary Jean, and from Peggy. Sent home a dozen snapshots from Australia. In the evening, I went to the show and saw *Up in Mabel's Room,* and boy was that a show and did they have some cracks in it.

Sunday, July 9, 1944

Well, it sure is nice to have an icebox. Good cold water and fruit juice. I now have eight men on my watch. Got fresh meat in again today and in the evening we went down to the docks and saw *Mr. and Mrs. North,* with Gracie Allen and she sure is a nitwit.

Monday, July 10, 1944

Well, they have secured Saipan. They're right on the ball. Got a letter from the folks, they have received my watch, ring, and money, etc. Put Charlie in as butcher now so our watch doesn't have meat to cut. Sent home some snapshots of Melbourne. Signed for a registered package. In the evening, I went to the show and saw *Costal Command,* a British picture.

Tuesday, July 11, 1944

Well, today I got four letters, two from Reta with some snaps in it and also a registered package with a like-in-it (Maori god good-luck charm), which was darn nice of her to send. One from Peggy, Val, and Jeanne. In the evening I went to the show at tanks and saw *The Navy Way.*

Wednesday, July 12, 1944

Well, I've got two and a half years in the service now. January will be three years. Then I'll start drawing 3% extra long dividends on my 26th month overseas. Boy, I got such a head cold, I feel sick as a dog and weak as a kitten. In the evening I went to the show and saw *Pin Up Girl,* with Betty Grable.

Thursday, July 13, 1944

Well, it rained like hell all night long. Hear no one is going home now until November. Sent home $100.00. Wrote a few letters. Doggie got caught early yesterday morning, oversexed. Had a hell of a hard day. Notice on the bulletin board, no more men are going home. Stayed in in the evening and read *The Courage of Marge O'Doone.*

Friday, July 14, 1944

Well, I got a couple of handkerchiefs from Reta today. Worked until noon then had to put in a request for the presidential election. They put out a tracer to try and get back the boys they sent home for the new battalion they're forming. Went to the show in the evening and saw *Shine on Harvest Moon,* good show. Rained like hell but I still didn't leave the show.

Saturday, July 15, 1944

Well, didn't do anything in the morning, just loafed around then went to work. Had quite a hard day but it's all in a day's work. In the evening I saw a really good picture. Cary Grant in *Destination Tokyo,* certainly a wonderful picture.

Sunday, July 16, 1944

Well, today was really a tough day for us. Two hundred twenty-four men came in. Amphibian boys, part of 3rd and part of the 4th Amphibian Tractor Battalion. Captain Fitzgerald is going to take over and make the 6th Amphibian Battalion out of it. Saw the show with Wallace Berry in *Salute to the Marines.* Came back, they had two Marines they found stealing officer's whiskey. One called the major a lying cocksucker. Division Military Police took them away. Hate to be in their shoes.

Monday, July 17, 1944

Beautiful day today. Wrote a letter to Betty Fisher. Heat rash is still pretty bad all over the upper half of my body. Itches like hell. Didn't go to the show, stayed in camp. Getting ready to move into the new galley. Played cards in the evening, broke even. Went to bed early as I was really tired.

Tuesday, July 18, 1944

Well, I worked until noon and then I hit the sack. I got a registered package from Peggy today. She finally got what I asked her for. Itch sure as hell isn't getting any better. In the evening I went to the dock and saw *Dixie Dugan.* Tomorrow *Bataan* is playing and I sure want to see it.

Wednesday, July 19, 1944

Well, we now have fifteen tractors to a platoon instead of ten; that makes fifty to a company. Went to work in our new galley. Boys going on maneuvers all the time and artillery is firing day and night. In the evening I went to the show and saw *Dixie Dugan.*

Thursday, July 20, 1944

Well, early this morning I really took a flop. Dark, no light. Result; one thick lip, uppercut halfway across, one cut jaw with swelling like an egg, one leg bruised form knee to hip. Can't bend it and minor scratches on arms and hands. Got in 26 new Buffaloes. Armored jobs with turrets, 37 MM and one air cooled .30 and two .50 calibers in back. Saw *This Above All.* Had seen it in Australia.

Friday, July 21, 1944

Well, the same old grind again today. Went to work at noon today. Worked until 6:30 P.M. In the evening I went to the show and saw *Make Way for Tomorrow;* it wasn't anything to brag about.

Saturday, July 22, 1944

Well, we had four tractors out all night long. One caught fire but they got them all in safely yesterday. Got hold of some real stateside whiskey, Calvert's. Collins had it and gave me a couple of shots. In the evening we went to the show and saw *Sahara,* with Humphrey Bogart and it sure was a swell picture.

Sunday, July 23, 1944

Started real nice today and ended up raining. Wrote a couple of letters. Mail came in but I didn't get any. What the hell's the difference; won't be here too much longer anyhow. The American force landed on Guam and has established a beachhead. In the evening I went to the show at tanks and saw *Seven Days Ashore.*

Monday, July 24, 1944

Well, it really rained all day long today. They brought some more new tractors in today. Received eight letters today and some snapshots of Reta. Stayed in during the evening and wrote some letters. The water is four to six inches deep around the tent and I can't see any more of this mud and rain than I have to.

Tuesday, July 25, 1944

Well, today it rained continuously all day long. Wrote some letters in the morning. Also, American Marines have landed on Tinian which is just below Saipan in the Mariana Islands. Really going to town now. In the evening I stayed in camp and read our new *Leatherneck Magazine* for men overseas only.

Wednesday, July 26, 1944

Well, I had 5:30 A.M. chow for around 250 men again going on maneuvers. That's been going on more every day for the last three weeks. Well, worked until noon. Hit the sack and in the evening I went to the show at Steel Pier and saw Henry Aldrich in *Boy Scout.* Met Bill from battalion and he told me one of the fellows I knew got killed at Gloucester, one died here, and one lost his eyesight from drinking.

Thursday, July 27, 1944

Well, artillery was firing all night long. Wrote a couple of letters. Got the news that our laundry has moved. Guess I'll have to do an awful lot of washing tomorrow. In the evening I went to the show and saw *Rosie the Riveter.*

Friday, July 28, 1944

Worked until noon today and then I went down and washed clothes until around 3:00 P.M. Got a letter from Norm today. In the evening I went down and saw the boxing matches. Picked six out of nine winners. Have to take an IQ test tomorrow.

Saturday, July 29, 1944

Told me I take my test Monday morning. Yes, this is inspection again as every week. Ought to hear from some of the boys pretty soon. In the evening Collins and I went to the show and saw Errol Flynn in *Uncertain Glory,* which I certainly enjoyed but didn't like the ending of the picture.

Sunday, July 30, 1944

Well, it started out raining and did quite a bit of it. Worked till noon. Washed clothes. Got a letter from Marguerite and then went to the docks and saw Ida Lupino in *The Hard Way,* which she played a very good role and also saw Cary Grant and Ginger Rogers in *Once Upon a Honeymoon.* Didn't get back to camp till around 11:15 P.M.

Monday, July 31, 1944

Well, last day in July. Greater part of the morning was spent taking an IQ test. Then Bill and I went to the show and saw *Major of 44th Street,* and came back to camp and saw about my pictures. I get them Wednesday night, so he says.

Tuesday, August 1, 1944

Well, here we go on another month. Wonder what September holds in store or maybe even this month? Washed clothes again. Got a letter from Betty Fisher and Reta. Get my pictures tomorrow. In the evening I went to the show and saw *The Harrigan Kid* with Collins and then retired.

Wednesday, August 2, 1944

The admiral and the general are coming here today. Lot of scuttlebutt that we're leaving but soon. Can't survey clothes any more. Outfits are starting to pack up. In the evening we went to the show and saw *This Is the Life;* also I got my pictures; they came out but none too good.

Thursday, August 3, 1944

Well, today we got three shots: smallpox vaccination in upper left arm, cholera in left forearm, and tetanus in upper right arm, and two more to get next week. Sent laundry out as it started raining once more. Received a letter from the folks and Margaret and one from Betty Fisher. In the early part of the afternoon I hit the sack, that is, 5:00 P.M.

Friday, August 4, 1944

Well, the morning just passed and nothing accomplished. Got rid of some excess gear and then I went on watch. Worked until 6:00 P.M., then I went to the show and saw *Three Men in White,* and came back to camp and saw I had some letters from Reta. Then I read a little while and hit the sack.

Saturday, August 5, 1944

Well, Saturday morning, inspection day again. Boy, what a day; worked half the morning cleaning up the galley and then it was called off. Sent home the pictures I got here. Also got a letter from Tebbe, the rest of the boys are on their way out here. Saw *Gaslight* in the evening with Charles Boyer and it sure was good.

Sunday, August 6, 1944

Well, it started out to be another beautiful Sunday. Wrote a few letters. Sent a snapshot to Marguerite and one to Reta. Didn't go to the show in the evening. 6:00 A.M. chow for the battalion as Bob Hope is going to be down at the dock at 9:00 A.M. Can't go as I have the duty. Bill Collins came over and we wrote letters.

Monday, August 7, 1944

Just two years ago today that we hit Guadalcanal, that's why Bob Hope is here today, for our anniversary. Also Jerry Colonna, Frances Langford, etc., but as I had the watch, I couldn't go! Got a letter from Reta with a couple of snapshots. In the evening I went to the show, *Sleepy Lagoon,* with Judy Canova, but as a show, it smelt.

Tuesday, August 8, 1944

Well, today I got a couple of letters from Peggy and some snapshots of her which are nice. Worked from noon on. I have to go to the range and fire the machine gun from the tractors. In the evening I just sat around and talked all evening.

Wednesday, August 9, 1944

Well, I worked until 6:00 A.M. then I went out to the machine gun range and fired the .30 caliber and the .50 caliber. Stationary firing from the tractor. Got a letter from Jean Oakley and one from home. Went to the show in the evening and saw *Girls in Washington,* which was a lousy picture.

Thursday, August 10, 1944

Well, I wrote a few letters in the morning and at noon I went to work. In the evening I stayed in camp and cooked off all my hams. The kid that worked on pots stole a fellow's watch and got a Summary Court Martial, busted from Private First Class to Private.

Friday, August 11, 1944

Well, I had to work till noon again. Just before dinner, one of the fellows dumped some boiling water on my leg. It's bandaged up but still doesn't feel too good. Slept a little and in the evening Bill and I went to the show and saw Edward G. Robinson in *Tampico,* with Lynn Bari and Victor McLaglen.

Saturday, August 12, 1944

Here we are, another Saturday and another inspection and then early chow and out to the rifle range. Shot pretty fair. About 1½ miles out to the range through the boondocks and then had to try and surprise an ambush that was laid for us. In the evening I stayed in camp and played cards. No mail again today.

Sunday, August 13, 1944

Well, it was another beautiful Sunday. Mail came in. I received a letter from Peggy. Got off at noon and hit the sack. There sure is a lot of scuttlebutt going around about the coming blitz. In the evening I went to the show and saw *Follow the Boys,* with George Raft.

Monday, August 14, 1944

Well, in the morning I got a letter from Peggy and then I wrote her and the folks. Went to work at noon, then in the evening I went to the show and saw *Edge of Darkness,* with Errol Flynn, which was a very good show.

Tuesday, August 15, 1944

Well, I worked until noon today and then in the afternoon I and three other fellows got a rubber boat and went over to the other island. Got some nice shells and caught two large-size fish. We were knee deep in water and chased them ashore. Also killed three coral snakes. Sure had a lot of fun. In the evening we went to the show and saw *What a Man,* which was certainly a swell picture.

Wednesday, August 16, 1944

Well, it won't be long now. Sure wish we would leave and get into action. Getting a good tan again. At 9:00 P.M. last night they announced that the Allies had landed in the southern part of France. It's funny the things that pass through a person's mind when you know you're going into action. Little things, things so incidental, things one thought one has long been forgotten. In the evening I drew 17 bottles of beer and drank a few and really felt it.

Thursday, August 17, 1944

Well, I worked until noon today. Mail came in; I got a V-mail from Dad. The commandant, General Vandergriff, was here today for a demonstration with our flame throwers. Drank a few more beers; lovely stuff, that beer. Then

I lay down for a while. Later on I went to the show. Show was called off so I sat around shooting the breeze. Bought a cigarette lighter for $7.00.

Friday, August 18, 1944

Well, here it is one more day closer to the blitz. No mail again today. Worked all afternoon. No more laundry going out. In the evening we went to the show but it was just shorts and they weren't very good so got up and came back. Had a couple of beers and hit the sack.

Saturday, August 19, 1944

Inspection day today. Worked until noon and then I washed clothes. Drew some more gear. Also I got a letter from Marguerite and pictures from Mother. In the evening we went to Steel Pier and saw Wallace Berry in *Wyoming* and *No Place for Women.* Didn't get back till around 11:30 P.M.

Sunday, August 20, 1944

Well, I'm a machine gunner in the first wave. We'll be leaving here before very long. Going on maneuvers to Cape Esperance off Guadalcanal. Didn't go to the show in the evening. Sold a set of pictures and got my gear all marked and drew new shelter half.

Monday, August 21, 1944

Well, they tell us we're going to leave here Thursday or Friday. I guess old Tojo will get a surprise next month; maybe we will too as far as that goes. In the evening I went to the show and saw *Sensations of 1945,* an official picture of our landing at Cape Gloucester.

Tuesday, August 22, 1944

Got a letter from Tebbe and one from Reta. Everybody is on edge and raring to go. The very air is seething with excitement. I sold a couple of sets of pictures. In the evening I stayed in camp and played cards but can't seem to concentrate on anything. Can't write any more letters.

Wednesday, August 23, 1944

Well, I worked until noon today and then packed some of my gear. Bedding and one pack and loaded it on the tractor. Some of the boys are going aboard tomorrow. Close officer's mess tomorrow. Also staff H Company tomorrow morning. I'll leave either tomorrow night or Friday morning. Stayed in camp and played cribbage. So we come one more day nearer our day. May God be with us all and spare as many as possible.

Thursday, August 24, 1944

Well, there was an awful lot of excitement today, everybody getting ready to go. They closed officer's mess and N Company mess today. Fed them all, now not quite a thousand men, lacking around 25 or 30. Saw *Gangster Touchy,* good show.

Friday, August 25, 1944

Well, noon chow is the last meal today. Finally going aboard ship. Well, closed the galley down and left at 2:00 P.M. Got down to the docks and didn't go aboard until around 7:30 P.M. Got two letters after I got on; one from Betty and the other from Mona and hit the sack.

Saturday, August 26, 1944

Didn't get up until around 9:30 A.M. Sure is going to be a lot of Amphibians on this blitz. Noon chow: roast beef, mashed potatoes, peas, bread, peaches, and water. Supper: two wieners, one stalk of celery, spoonful of lima beans, coffee, and a chocolate rations bar. Oh well, could always be worse, or could it? I guess we start maneuvers tomorrow as we're off to Guadalcanal now.

Back to Guadalcanal 12

Sunday, August 27, 1944

We got up at 2:30 A.M. this morning as we are going on maneuvers. Back here at Guadalcanal after two years; not much progress. Hell. Left the ship at around 7:30 A.M. and didn't get ashore until around 9:00 A.M. Made two trips with troops, went into the beach and stayed. Hotter than hell out in that water for over three hours in that sun. Went swimming in the Francis River on Cape Esperance and later on, in the ocean. Ate rations.

Monday, August 28, 1944

Left the ship around 7:30 A.M. and went down by Koli Point. Came back up a ways and gassed up on the island. Tomorrow is dress rehearsal with shelling and all. Live ammunition. Got back aboard ship around noon. We're going to bivouac on the island for three days. Didn't have to do anything after dinner but chain down the tractor.

Tuesday, August 29, 1944

Well, up at 2:30 A.M. again this morning. Had maneuvers, the last one before D-Day. Had ships shelling the beaches, planes bombing and strafing the beach. L.C.I. firing rockets really was something to see. Maneuvers came off pretty good. Came back aboard ship around 3:30 P.M. Going off the ship again tomorrow morning. Boy, what a day; hot, tired, dirty, and soaking wet.

Wednesday, August 30, 1944

Well, we went ashore around 9:00 A.M. Worked on the tractors, gassed up, went back to the ship for dinner chow and then back ashore. Cleaned rifle and machine guns and around 4:30 P.M. went back aboard ship leaving half the men ashore. Tomorrow we go ashore and they go back to the ship. Say we're going to get beer before we leave here. I sure hope so.

Thursday, August 31, 1944

Well, this morning we are at Tulagi to get stores and stuff, also got some fresh water off of a water tender that holds six million gallons of water. Guess we will be here all day and go over to Guadalcanal tomorrow. Also say we are going to get our beer tomorrow. Stayed in the hold most of the day. Read and slept as it was cool and raining all day long.

Friday, September 1, 1944

Well, we're back at Guadalcanal this morning. Raining and mud. Miserable as hell. Left the tractors and went up to the Red Cross and it was disgusting of course; there were women there and a couple of them pretty nice. Can get anything there for a price. Film $3.50 per roll. Necklaces $10.00. Jap bills, three for $10.00. Regular stands where they sell Jap souvenirs. What a racket!

Saturday, September 2, 1944

Well, we got mail. I got seven letters and a couple of sugar reports. Came back aboard ship around 1:00 P.M., dirty and wet as per usual. Stay dry now until D-Day. Guess we'll be here a couple of more days yet. 5th Amphibians were aboard ship and I heard that seven LSTs blew up in Pearl Harbor so they lost all their tractors. Can't see anything but blitz ahead for us. Live through one, go into another.

Sunday, September 3, 1944

Well, this is our last day here at Guadalcanal. Never thought we would see this place two years later. We were supposed to leave here tomorrow but instead we're supposed to leave under way tonight at 2200, that's 10:00 P.M. So the hand of fate reaches out once more. Got mail. I received a letter from Betty Fisher and one from Peggy and my old pal Tom. Wrote some letters even though they can't be mailed.

Destination Peleliu Island 13

Monday, September 4, 1944

Well, here's one more day nearer D-Day and that much less time the Japs have before they lose another island. Well, we didn't get under way last night. We just got under way at 0900. Off to the races. Some ship this is, water isn't on half the time, the head is either closed or else the water isn't on so it might just as well be closed. Talk about rough weather, we got it up on deck waiting for chow and a wave came over the side and soaked me.

Tuesday, September 5, 1944

Well, it isn't quite so rough this morning. At least not like it was yesterday. Major says we are all to be relieved by November—of course you have to live through it. Three air craft carriers (converts) came real close to us yesterday. Hit the sack early as ship is darkened around 6:45 P.M.

Wednesday, September 6, 1944

Well, we set the time back a half hour yesterday, or I should say, late last night. Washed clothes and cleaned my M-1 in the morning and in the afternoon I finished my book, *The Tragedy of the Hollow,* and then I wrote a few letters. Hit the sack early in the evening as per usual.

Thursday, September 7, 1944

Heard today that the Allies are ten miles in Germany along a 100 mile front. Late last night we ran into a hell of a storm. On deck the water was over your shoes. The major is reported to have said that we will be relieved by

November. Just hope that all our boys pull through this so they can go home. Was duty NCO today and Sergeant of the Guard and have the duty till after breakfast tomorrow.

Friday, September 8, 1944

From the scuttlebutt, one week from today is D-Day! Weather isn't too bad, the sun was out this morning for a change and it was a nice day all day long. Read a little. Had the duty till after breakfast. Finished reading my book. Ran the tractors for awhile in the afternoon. Then spent the remainder of the afternoon playing cribbage.

Saturday, September 9, 1944

Well, late last night it got pretty rough. Time is still being set back ½ hour per day for the last four days. I suppose the same thing will happen again tonight at 7:30 P.M. At 11:30 P.M. we had an air raid but it was a friendly plane. At 4:00 A.M. General Quarters went but there was no action. The gunners then all had A.A. practice and these gunners are pretty good. Ate supper at 3:30 P.M. Long time from supper to breakfast. Darken ship at 5:30 P.M. last night.

Sunday, September 10, 1944

Five days to go. Getting restless and so are the men to some extent. Well, I really started playing cribbage in earnest today and I like it. It doesn't seem to grow monotonous no matter how much you play it. Finished reading *Trail's End,* and I am now reading *H. M. Pulham, Esquire,* which isn't bad so far as I've read.

Monday, September 11, 1944

Well, it was a nice day all day long. Rained early part of this morning. Turned all our mail in today. But it won't go out until after D-Day. We played cribbage nearly all day. Breaks in between for chow. Won 14 out of 18 games. Had to run the tractors again today.

Tuesday, September 12, 1944

Well, we got some good news on the radio that a Jap convoy was sunk off the Philippines; a 50 ship convoy and then it was posted on the bulletin board that 83 ships were sunk and that 85 tons of bombs were dropped on Peleliu in the Palau Islands where we're going to hit. Also the Navy supposed to start shelling them today.

Wednesday, September 13, 1944

Well, they should be giving them hell now, bombing and shelling both. Had General Alarm, General Quarters air raid, everything all day long, but as far as we know, nothing happened. Well, won't be much longer now, I guess this is D-Day minus two.

Thursday, September 14, 1944

Well, got the machine guns all oiled up, ammo dried out, oiled and put in cases. Getting squared away now. Issued ammo for small arms and hand grenades. Late last night news: 120 tons of bombs dropped on Palau Islands in the last two days. Japanese garrison evacuating Palau Island. Well, we're all set to go tomorrow; reveille goes at 2:30 A.M.

Friday, September 15, 1944

D-Day has been changed till tomorrow the 16th. So of course everybody was doing a lot of things that they had forgotten before and of course weapons were given special attention.

D-Day at Peleliu Island 14

Saturday, September 16, 1944

Well, we got up at 2:30 A.M. Now 6:45 A.M. We're going off at 7:30 A.M. God, what a bombardment the Navy has thrown down so far. This shouldn't be too tough. Now, today first time I've had to record events. Went in on the 5th wave and we just about got in and they let us have it with mortars, machine guns, rifles. One landed right beside us. Dave got shrapnel through his helmet and debris flew in the cargo compartment. Took three men out with us that were shot up pretty bad. Then back in again into that inferno hell with the 12th wave. Tractors that got hit when we went in first were burning and smoking. Hell of a sight. Then back again with the 16th wave. Scaredest I've ever been. Casualties were high, and then we hauled ammo and water and mortars and 40-MM guns. Then we loaded up with 1½ tons of TNT and nitro as men needed stuff bad. Got about thirty yards from shore and damn if they didn't throw down a mortar barrage. They were hitting on both sides of us. When we hit the beach, we left that tractor like a bullet. Then we took chow in and some clown lit a match out in the open as it was dark then. Then they really let loose with mortars again. Went out about 150 yards off shore to spend the night as they were using flares; we could easily be seen and they opened up on us. This happened three times at daylight again till we moved out of range.

Sunday, September 17, 1944

How I came through all of that alive, I'll never figure out. Found out we lost nine tractors out of my company alone. Bertaine got killed, Rosil, Hogan from C Company. Suds by a mortar. Hazel got hit bad. Price got hit. Donahey. Two men missing. Bivins got hit this morning. 1st Regiment has about one company left. K Company has nine men left. So far around 3,000 casualties.

Mortar fire was bad again today. Japs took the air field back four times last night. Crosley and Brown cracked up. Dead lying all over the beach. Japs and Marines alike and smell terrible. Saw one Marine with his head blown off, one arm, and the rest of his body in half. All day long was hell. Around 7:00 P.M. we got aboard LST 27, repair ship as our tracks were broken halfway through. Staying aboard here tonight and get some sleep, thank God, and leave at 5:30 A.M. tomorrow morning.

Monday, September 18, 1944

Well, this is the third day here and hell is really flying. Ikeham got killed, so did Kent. Kromberger, Falkenham, Hilman got wounded and evacuated. I got a Jap mortar, a BAR, a couple of bayonets, and a couple of rifles. Dead men lying all over, we have been running over them all the time.

Tuesday, September 19, 1944

Well, we had some bad links but they needed TNT up at the front so we took it up. They told us if we got back, they would fix our tractor up. Made it OK and most of the day was spent repairing the bloody tractor.

Wednesday, September 20, 1944

Well, this is really a blitz; it's said to be worse than Saipan, Guam, or Tarawa. On Tokyo radio they announced that this is the bloodiest battle of the Pacific. I never saw as many dead men lying around in all my life. Worked right up on the front lines all day long with Charlie Company 1st Battalion 1st Marines and the boys were really catching hell. Was under small arms fire.

Thursday, September 21, 1944

Well, today we worked all day long for Charlie Company, 1st Battalion, 1st Marines and hell was really flying around up there. A 90-MM mortar had 2nd Company pinned down; it landed two rounds down on the beach, hit an ammo dump, and wounded 80 men. But our boys in Charlie Company knocked him out. Haven't had time to pick up any souvenirs to speak of outside of a few weapons.

Friday, September 22, 1944

Well, we worked all day long with I, K, and L Companies, 3rd Battalion, 1st Marines. There sure has been a hell of a lot of casualties. A sniper knocked off three men right in front of us on our way up to the front. I found some Japanese campaign ribbons and a coin, that's about all.

Saturday, September 23, 1944

Well, we didn't go up to the front lines at all today, they had us carrying 105s and 155s all day long. God, I'm so tired it seems each morning when I get up, I'm tireder than I was the night before. Hear our major is going back to the States. Big deal.

Sunday, September 24, 1944

Well, they took me off the tractor this morning and we're starting to set up a galley. Cleaned up my mortar a little. Major is leaving tomorrow and Captain Nooman is now our battalion commander. He should be a good one. So far there have been 800 killed and 4,000 wounded. B Company has had 27 wounded boys. Boys now have the Japs all in one pocket and are throwing everything at them.

Merle Fisher was wounded sometime after his last entry of September 24 and died of his wounds aboard the USS *Solace* on September 26, 1944.

Front row, sitting, fifth from right.

March 26, 1942

Sonny New River, N.C.

Feb. 1942

Paris Island

April 1942

New River N. C.

April 26, 1942

Sonny Amph. Tractor
Deerfield Point

Back row, third from right.